Excel

BASIC SKILLS

ENGLISH

YEAR 4

AGES 9–10

ENGLISH WORKBOOK

Get the Results You Want!

Jane Baker

PASCAL PRESS

Reprinted 2006, 2007, 2009, 2010 (twice), 2012, 2013, 2016, 2018, 2020, 2022

ISBN 978 1 74125 157 9

Pascal Press
PO Box 250
Glebe NSW 2037
(02) 8585 4050
www.pascalpress.com.au

Publisher: Vivienne Joannou
Series developer: Kristine Brown
Project editor: Emma Driver
Edited by Christine Eslick
Page design and layout by Jelly Design
Typesetting by Alena Jencik, Grand Graphix Pty Ltd
Cover by DiZign Pty Ltd
Photos by Photodisc and Photos.com
Printed by Vivar Printing/Green Giant Press

Contents

Acknowledgements

The author and publisher would like to thank the following copyright holders for permission to print their Year 4 writings: Stephanie Compton, Jim Baker, Anthea Compton and Penny Baker.

The assistance of teachers of the South Coast region of New South Wales is gratefully acknowledged, particularly that of Mrs Rhonda Basset, Acting Principal of Binalong Public School.

To the student

When you use this book you will be practising recognising and writing many of the text types you learn at school. Several of the sample texts have been written by students in Year 4 and are good examples of what a Year 4 student can achieve.

Carefully read the sample text at the beginning of each chapter. Check what special features of the writing the arrows point to as you read. Then work through the questions and the exercises that follow.

Work through the chapters in order, from one to eleven. This will allow you to build on the skills learned in one chapter in the next chapter. By the end of the year you will have a good understanding of Year 4 English.

You will need a good dictionary (e.g. a small *Macquarie* or *Collins Australian* dictionary) and a folder to keep your writing safe and clean, as well as a quiet place with good light in which to work.

Good luck and have fun.

Jane Baker

Chapter 1 Writing a recount

When we write a **recount** we are telling **what happened in sequence**. This recount comes from the diary of a trip to New Zealand.

STRUCTURE

LANGUAGE

Our trip to New Zealand

Orientation tells time and place

On Thursday we crossed the Southern Alps. It took hours. We drove through Arthurs Pass and then stopped to look at the mountains. The peaks looked a bit like black and white pictures, with their bright white snow and big black rocks. We stayed overnight in Greymouth, where we bought some books.

Comparison helps reader to "see" the peaks

Sequenced events in paragraphs

Yesterday we drove on to see the famous Franz Josef Glacier. First we left our things in our motel and then we set out to walk to the glacier. It took a long, long time to walk over the stones in the bottom of the valley and when we got to the wall of the glacier we were very thirsty. We broke off a tiny bit of glacial ice and sucked it. We were drinking water that was thousands of years old. It was much nicer than sucking ice from the fridge.

Time word to make sequence clear

Personal comments on facts

Today we drove to the Fox Glacier. Someone had told Dad about a lake on the way so we went there first. We had to walk through a dark forest to find Lake Matheson. It was a very cold lake because all its water came from the glacier.

By the time we got to the Fox Glacier valley it was too late in the day to reach the glacier itself. We stayed in the car park to watch great big green-brown parrots called keas. They were vicious. They were walking all over the cars in the car park, ripping up soft parts with their beaks. They chewed up windscreen wipers. We even saw one pecking the air valves on tyres to let them down.

Good choice of adjective

Examples of viciousness

Conclusion looks forward to next stage of journey

Tomorrow we have to get up early because we are flying to the top of Franz Josef in a ski-plane. I am looking forward to that because the top of the glacier is all deep snow. So far we have only seen the front ends of glaciers and they are like huge walls of blue-green ice with brown streaks in them.

Time word

Interesting comparison

Penny (aged 9)

What did you read?

1. **Circle** the correct answer. Crossing the Southern Alps did not take very long. **True/False**

2. **Circle** the correct answer. The travellers stayed overnight in:
   a Arthurs Pass b Greymouth c Lake Matheson

3. **Circle** the correct answer. The thirsty travellers drank icy water from:
   a Lake Matheson b Fox Glacier c Franz Josef Glacier

4. **Circle** the correct answer. The water in Lake Matheson comes from:
   a a glacier b a river c the sea

5. **Circle** the most complete answer. Keas:
   a look like green-brown parrots
   b are large green parrots with big beaks
   c look like big green-brown parrots
   d look like big parrots and have vicious habits

6. **Explain** in your own words what you would see at the end of a glacier.

   ____

   ____

7. If the ice is blue-green because it is so deep and thick, can you **work out** why it has brown streaks in it? (*Clue:* Think about what the glacier is moving through.)

   ____

   ____

How is it written?

1. Time words (adverbs of time) make the sequence (order of happening) clear. **Write** at least two time words used in the text:

   a ________________ b ________________

2. Recounts are usually written in the past. **Find** three verbs written in the **past** in the first paragraph.

   a ________________ b ________________ c ________________

3. In the first paragraph the writer has used a comparison to help us see the mountain peaks. **Complete** this comparison: They looked a bit like ______________________________.

4. Recount writing contains facts. **Write** one fact about keas that you find in paragraph 4.

   ____

Spelling and meaning

sequence	bought	peak	tire
diary	brought	peek	tiring
dairy	glacier	glacial	tyre

When you learn spelling, **look** at the word, **cover** the word, **write** the word and **check** your spelling. Do this as often as it takes to get it right.

1 Some words look very like other words with completely different meanings. **Circle** the correct word in these sentences.

a Eddie **bought/brought** a book on glaciers from the new bookshop.
b It is not polite to **peak/peek** at birthday presents early.
c Lucy writes in her **diary/dairy** every morning.
d Snow chains prevent car **tyres/tires** from skidding in deep snow.
e Mt Kosciusko is 2228 metres high at its **peek/peak**.
f New Zealand is famous for its **diary/dairy** cows and their cream.

2 **Sequence** means "in order". Read these lists. If they are in correct sequence **write *Y*** in the space provided. If they are out of sequence **write *N***.

a Dressing: coat, shirt, trousers, socks ________
b Apple-eating: remove seeds, peel, eat ________
c Mowing: start mower, cut grass, put petrol in tank ________
d Catch bus: board bus, pay fare, find seat, sit down ________

3 The sound ***er*** (*glacier*) can be spelt in many ways (e.g. ***ea**rly*, c***ur**ly*, s***ir***, w***or**ld*). Can you **complete** this table?

ER	**IR**	**UR**	**EAR**
H __ __ D (cows)	WH __ __ L (spin)	F __ __ (cat coat)	H __ __ __ D (the ear did it)
F __ __ N (a plant)	B __ __ D (sparrow)	F __ __ L (to roll a flag)	P __ __ __ L (jewel)

4 **Label** the following pictures with a word from the table above.

a ____________________

b ____________________

c ____________________

Grammar

A **simple sentence** contains a subject, a verb and an object.

Example **Penny** (subject) **explored** (verb) **the glacier** (object).

A **compound sentence** contains two or more equally important **Subject → Verb → Object** patterns joined by ***and***, ***or*** or ***but***.

Examples Penny explored the glacier **but** her mother studied plants **and** her father took photographs.

The travellers could climb to the top of the glacier **or** they could fly there.

1 **Underline** the subject, **circle** the verb and **double underline** the object in each of these sentences.

a Glaciers are rivers of ice.

b Harry climbed the glacier wall.

c A glacier climber carries rope, spikes and a small hammer.

2 **Rearrange** the words in each exercise to form a **complete simple sentence**.

a very cold mountain lakes The waters of are ______________________

b Snowboarding popular sports in the Alps and skiing are ______________________

____

c very thin Mountain air is ______________________

3 **Join** these simple sentences to make compound sentences using ***and*** or ***but***.

a Glaciers carry stones in their ice. Rivers carry silt in their waters.

____

b Glaciers begin in alpine lakes. Rivers begin in mountain rains.

____

c Thin ice looks white. Thick ice looks blue or green.

____

Punctuation

Sentences start with a **capital letter** and so do proper nouns (special names of people and places such as ***Julia*** and ***Egypt***) and titles (e.g. ***Doctor***, ***General***).

Example **S**ir **E**dmund **H**ilary and **T**enzing **N**orgay were the first people to reach the peak of **M**t **E**verest.

Insert all the necessary capital letters in this passage.

some mountains are famous for their snow, mountains like everest in nepal, fuji in japan, the matterhorn in austria and tongariro in new zealand. other mountains like mt st helen in the united states, vesuvius in italy, pinatubo in the philippines and gunung agung in indonesia are volcanic and famous for boiling lava and explosions.

Fun with words

1 This is a Chill Factor Scale. Can you **arrange** the words in the box on this scale from warmer at the bottom to colder at the top?

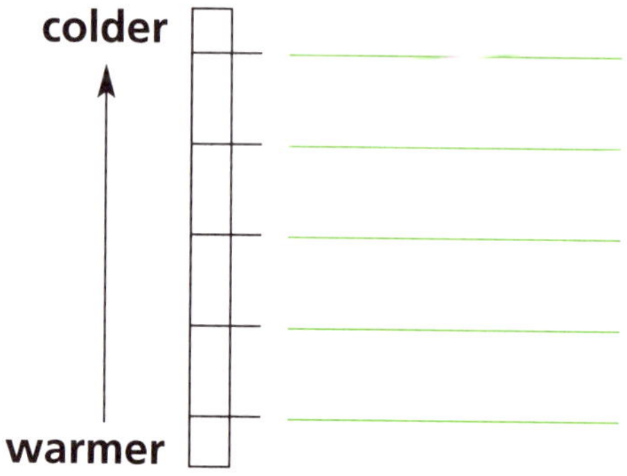

cold
chilly
mild
icy
cool

2 **Choose** a word from the Chill Factor Scale that best describes these scenes.

a ____________ b ____________ c ____________

3 These are all water words. Can you **complete** them?

a a river of ice: _ _ _ C _ _ _

b a body of water on land: L _ K _

c a boomerang-shaped lake near a river: B _ L L _ B _ NG

d the ebb and flow of water on the beach: T _ _ E

4 Getting around in alpine country (high snowy mountain country) requires special vehicles and equipment. Can you **unscramble** the names of these alpine vehicles and tools?

KISS	long narrow footwear for snow travel	S__________
DELS	dog-drawn cart on steel runners	S__________
GGANTOBO	a small downhill speedster	T______________
AIRCH FILT	a seated lift up the mountain	C_________ _____

5 Who am I? I am an animal with four legs. I have a hairy coat and a beard. I have handsome curling horns and I am famous for my ability to climb steep mountain sides. I eat tiny alpine plants and summer grasses. My wife, strangely, is called Nanny even though I am young and so is she.

I am a _ _ _ _ _ _ _ _ _ _ _ _ _.

Your turn to write

Tip for top writers

When writing a recount, **list** all the events in the correct sequence. Then **write** your recount in that order.

1 **List** these morning events in their **correct sequence**.

eat	1.
wake	2.
dress	3.
wash	4.
clean teeth	5.

2 Look at Jenny's sequence of events. Can you help her **put** them in the **correct order** so she can recount how she got stuck up a tree.

I climbed higher	1.
Cat climbed higher	2.
Cat raced up tree	3.
Dog chased my cat	4.
Cat wouldn't come down	5.
I climbed tree	6.
Both too frightened to climb down	7.

3 Choose **two** of these topics and write a **sequence of events** for each.

a When I fell in the river   b When the truck tipped over   c When I spilt the milk

_______________   _______________

_______________   _______________

_______________   _______________

4 **Read** the sequences you wrote in question 3 again. **Choose** the most interesting one and then **write** a recount of what happened on a sheet of your own paper. Proofread it for spelling and punctuation errors. Make sure you have not used the same word too often, then write a neat clean copy and put it in your writing folder.

Chapter 2 Writing a narrative

When we write a **narrative** we are telling a story. It can be an imaginative story like this one or one set in the real world.

STRUCTURE

LANGUAGE

The Great Biscuit War

Introduction

July 16. This is the date that marks the signing of the peace treaty that ended five days of total war, the Great Biscuit War.

The war in sequence of battles

It all started when the 53rd Tim Tam Regiment was ambushed by the 19th Battalion of Chocolate Wheatens and heavily defeated. This caused an immediate declaration of war by the High Command of the Tim Tam army.

The first battle took place outside the headquarters of the 96th Division of Cavalry Crackers. It was a decisive Wheaten victory and the headquarters were overrun.

All the early battles went the same way until the 18th Wheaten Regiment attacked the encamped 44th Iced VoVo Division. Messengers were sent at once to gather the newly formed 42nd Home Made Armoured Battalion.

By the time the Home Mades arrived the Iced VoVos, who were hard pressed and had lost a lot of their icing, were beginning to falter.

But then the tide of battle and, indeed, the tide of war turned. Wheaten weapons were all but useless against the armour of the 42nds.

More Home Made Armoured Divisions were formed. All attempts to destroy them failed. Soon the Tim Tam army had surrounded the Wheaten capital and laid siege to it.

Resolution and conclusion

However, Wheaten defences were much too strong for Tim Tams to risk a direct attack so there was a stalemate and eventually, on July 15, peace talks began.
The very next day an agreement was reached and now the Great Biscuit War has faded into history.

Jim (aged 9)

Military words to make story sound real

Imaginative titles (names)

Good choice of verbs

Interesting phrases

What did you read?

1 **Circle** the correct answer:
July 16 was the day the Great Biscuit War started. **True/False**

2 Who started the war? ______________________________

3 **Name** the two sides in the war:
a the ______________ army b the ______________ army

4 **Circle** the correct word.
All the early battles were **victories/defeats** for the Tim Tams.

5 **Circle** the correct answer. The tide of battle changed:
a after the Cavalry Crackers' headquarters battle
b when the 88th Wheaten Regiment attacked the encamped Iced VoVos
c when the Armoured Home Mades entered the war

6 **Circle** the correct answer. The Tim Tam Army ***laid siege*** to the Wheaten capital. This means:
a The walls of the capital were attacked but could not be entered.
b The capital was entered by the Tim Tams.
c The capital was burned.

7 **Circle** the correct answer. The war lasted:
a fifteen days b five days c six days

How is it written?

1 **Circle** the correct answer. The story starts with a date and tells us the war lasted five days.
This orientation:
a gives us a time frame for the story
b needs more information
c is not important in the story

2 **Complete** this sentence.
The writer has described the battles of the war in S ___ QU ___ ___ CE.

3 The writer gives a military feel to his story by using technical words that soldiers use.
Write three examples of these words from the text.

a ______________ b ______________ c ______________

4 This is a humorous story. What makes it funny? **Circle** the two most correct answers.
a use of biscuit brand names for army units
b funny things that happen in the story
c description of the losses suffered by the Iced VoVos (their icing)

5 **Circle** the correct answer. The writer links the end of his story to the beginning of his story:
a with the peace treaty b with the Wheaten defences c with the stalemate

Spelling and meaning

sign	**armour**	**headquarters**	**weapon**
siege	**capital**	**falter**	**declaration**
icing	**biscuit**	**useless**	**decisive**

To make some long words easier to spell we can break them into two words (e.g. head/quarters).
Other long words we can break into **syllables** for easier spelling (e.g. cap/i/tal).

1 **Break** each of these words into **syllables**.

a biscuit ____________________ b icing ____________________

c falter ____________________ d declaration ____________________

e decisive ____________________ f useless ____________________

2 Dictionaries are valuable tools for writers. To use them you must know how to arrange words alphabetically.

a **Arrange** these words according to where their **first** letter comes in the alphabet:

capital	armour	biscuit

____

b If the first letters are the same, arrange the words according to their **second** letters. **Arrange** these words alphabetically:

division	defeat	dangerous

____

c Using the rules above, **number** these pictures 1–4 as they occur in the alphabet.

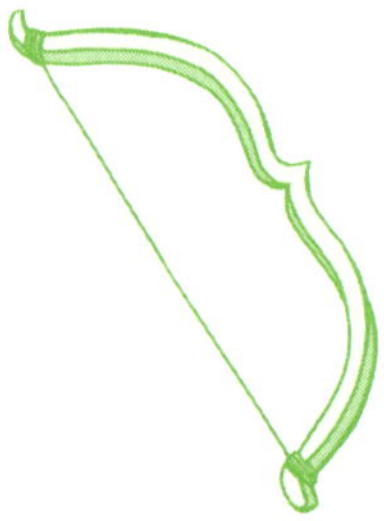

__________ __________ __________ __________

d If the first and second letters are the same, look at the **third** letters. **Arrange** these words alphabetically:

sign	siege	single

____

e Using all the rules above, **arrange** these words as you would find them in a dictionary:

falter	weapon	decisive	declaration	useless

____

3 **Insert** a word from the word box in each of these sentences. You can use a word twice.

a Canberra is the ______________ of Australia and Jakarta is the ______________ of Indonesia.

b Blue Line Shipping is an international company but its ______________ are in Wellington, New Zealand.

c A crab can use its claws as a ______________.

d Even a war horse will ______________ in its stride if it sees a rabbit jump out in front of it.

4 ***~our*** is a common spelling pattern (e.g. *arm**our***). Can you **complete** these ***~our*** words?

a Making jokes and being funny: H ___ MOUR

b Very loud noises all together: CL ___ MOUR

c Strength and good health: V ___ GOUR

Grammar

Nouns name things. There are many kinds of nouns. You already know about common nouns (e.g. gate, friend, house) and proper nouns (e.g. John, Korea, July).

Here are two more types of nouns.

Group or **collective nouns** are words that name a whole **group** of creatures or things.

Examples a regiment of soldiers, a flock of sheep

Abstract nouns name **ideas** and **feelings** (things we all know exist but cannot see).

Examples bravery, happiness, victory

1 **Name** the kind of underlined nouns in these sentences.

a Police and firefighters are well known for their courage. ______________

b The battalion marched across the parade ground. ______________

c A swarm of bees has settled in that big tree. ______________

d The choir sang with such sweetness the audience wept.

______________ ______________ ______________

2 **Insert** a group noun from the box below in each sentence. You will not need all the words.

congregation	school	pack	mob	flock	fleet	herd	clutch

a A ______________ of grey kangaroos dozed among the trees.

b The ______________ of wolves loped silently across the snow.

c A cyclone scattered the ______________ of yachts.

d A ______________ of tiny fish swirled in the waters off the reef.

e The church ______________ all enjoyed the Christmas service.

3 **Circle** all the abstract nouns in these sentences.

a Mr Venturini was known for his generosity to people in need.
b An army commander must show leadership in the field.
c The warrior showed mercy to his enemy.
d A true gentleman is known for his courtesy to everyone.

Punctuation

Sentences end with a **full stop** (**.**) if they **tell** us something. They end with a **question mark** (**?**) if they **ask** something and they end with an **exclamation mark** (**!**) if they express a **sudden emotion** like surprise or alarm.

Examples Australian and New Zealand soldiers fought at Gallipoli**.**
How many islands are there in Indonesia**?**
Ouch**!** Ouch**!** It hurts**!**

Insert all the missing punctuation.

a Is India north or south of the Equator
b Good heavens That pink pig is flying
c Chile's flag is sky blue with a big yellow sun in the middle
d What is the national language of Brazil

Fun with words

1 Can you **match** these groups with the group noun that names them?

a lions		swarm
b chickens		team
c people in church		clutch
d bees		pack
e wolves		congregation
f footballers		pride

2 You can have great fun inventing new group nouns (e.g. a **giggle** of girls, a **boast** of boys, an **argument** of lawyers). See if you can **invent** group nouns to name these groups. Think about what the groups do most together.

a a ________________ of teachers

b a ________________ of ducks

c a ________________ of racing cars

d a ________________ of gossips

e a ________________ of snakes

3 In an army some people have more authority than others. They have titles to show their place in the line of authority. The same happens in all organisations. Can you **arrange** these people in order of authority in their organisations, with the **most important person first**.

a sailors: seaman, admiral, captain

____

b school people: deputy, student, teacher, principal

____

c government people: minister, member of Parliament, prime minister

____

4 I am Godfrey of Lincolnshire. **Colour** me grandly for battle and label me by writing all the words in the chest next to the thing they describe.

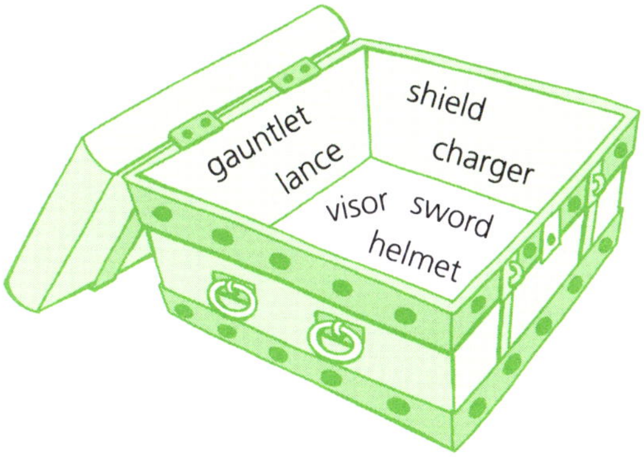

JOKE

Q. Why are police strong?

A. They can hold up a line of traffic with one hand.

Your turn to write

Tip for top writers

When writing a narrative:

- **Plan** your narrative (orientation, complication, resolution).
- **Sequence** the events (complication).
- Then **write** the story.

1 Claudia is writing a narrative about someone being lost in the bush. In the story the day turned cold and wet and her character, Mr Ibrahim, lost his way in the mist.
Write an **orientation** that would suit Claudia's narrative.

2 Johnny Imahera wants to write the story of a guitar competition in which his character, Jason Jackson, won an electric guitar. He has got as far as writing about Jason playing in the competition on a borrowed guitar.
Write a **resolution** that would fit his narrative.

3 **Choose** one of the following topics and **plan** a narrative about it on the scaffold below.

a The Water Slide Wars   b Beating the Bully   c The Duck Wins!

Orientation

Complication (sequenced events)

Resolution

4 On your own paper write the narrative according to your plan. Then proofread it. Put it in your writing folder for safekeeping.

Chapter 3 Writing humorous verse

Poems that are funny usually have a **regular rhythm** (beat) and a **regular pattern of rhyming words**. Limericks are a famous kind of humorous verse.

STRUCTURE

LANGUAGE

A selection of limericks

1
There once was a boy with a pain
Who said it's a pity again
Whenever I'm sick
It's surely a trick
There's either no school or no rain.

2
There was a farmer from Leeds
Who ate a packet of seeds.
It soon came to pass
He was covered in grass
And couldn't sit down for the weeds.
Sumhika Rao

3
There was an old rat we called Matt
Who was round, roly-poly and fat.
He saw a cat lurking
Was too slow from not working
And now it's the cat that is fat.

4
There was a young lady from Ryde.
Of eating green apples she died.
Inside the lamented
The apples fermented
And made cider inside her inside.

5
A flea and a fly in a flue
Were imprisoned, so what would they do?
Said the fly, "let us flee!"
"Let us fly," said the flea,
So they flew through a flaw in the flue.
Ogden Nash

6
There once was a lady named Lynn
Who was uncommonly thin.
When she assayed
To drink lemonade
She slipped through the straw and fell in.

7
There was an Old Man with a beard
Who said, "It's just as I feared!
Two Owls and a Hen,
Four Larks and a Wren
Have all built their nests in my beard!"
Edward Lear

Five lines

A common introduction

First and second lines rhyme—called rhyming couplets

Rhymes in lines 1, 2 and 5

Rhymes in lines 3 and 4

Clever rhyme right through if you say this aloud

Means "tried"

Clever use of ***fl*** words

What did you read?

1. **Circle** the correct answer. The schoolboy feels:
   a cheated b that life is unfair c both of the above

2. **Explain** how you think the man from Leeds ended up unable to sit down "because of the weeds".

   ____

   ____

3. **Write** one sentence explaining what happened to Matt, the rat.

   ____

4. **Where** did the apple-eating girl live? ____________________

5. **Circle** the correct answer. The word ***lamented*** means:
   a people grieved over her death
   b she was very sick

6. **Write** the product you get when apples are fermented. ________________

7. **Circle** the correct answer. The two trapped creatures in Ogden Nash's limerick were:
   a a fly and a flue b a flea and a flaw
   c a fly and a flea d a flee and a flue

8. **Write** what happened to Lynn. ______________________________

   ____

9. **Complete** this sentence.
   All the creatures that nested in the old man's beard were B ___ ___ ___ ___.

How is it written?

1. **Read** all the limericks carefully, and then **complete** the following sentence.
   The first line of a limerick always introduces the P ___ RS ___ N the limerick is about.

2. **Circle** two correct answers. The second line of a limerick tells us:
   a what the person of line 1 did or said
   b something about the person in line 1
   c nothing important

3. The first two lines and the last line of a limerick always **rhyme**. **Write** the rhyming words of lines 1, 2 and 5 in limerick 4.

   ______________ ______________ ______________

Spelling and meaning

either	pain	flea	flaw	lament
packet	wren	flee	flue	ferment
lurking	could	flew	beard	lemonade

Take care with **homophones** (words that sound the same but are spelt differently and have different meanings, such as ***flee*** and ***flea***).
Check your **dictionary** if you are not sure what any word means.

1 **Circle** the right answer to these questions.
 a Which one can bite you? **flee/flea**
 b Which one blows smoke? **flew/flue**
 c Which one is a fault or a weakness in something? **flaw/floor**

2 The word ***lurking*** suggests a **bad** intention in someone waiting and watching. The cat in limerick 3 was watching Matt the rat with a very bad intention, wasn't he?
Underline all the words in the following list that also suggest a **bad** intention:

sneak	look	spy	watch	creep	tell	tattle	take	rob

3 **Insert** the correct word from the list in question 2 in these sentences. You will not need all the words in the list.
 a Some beetles ________________ very slowly over the ground.
 b In the old days highwaymen used to ________________ people of their belongings.
 c A burglar must ________________ quietly into houses to avoid capture.
 d I like to ________________ the boats on the harbour.

4 **Insert** a word from the word box in these sentences.
 a A vintner will ________________ grape juice to make wine.
 b We will ________________ go swimming or go fishing.
 c The bruise from that cricket ball is causing me a lot of ________________.
 d Australia's fairy ________________ has beautiful blue feathers.
 e A cartoon pirate usually has red hair and a red ________________.

5 The word ***wren*** begins with a **silent *w***.
These words all begin with a **silent *w***. Can you **complete** them?
 a a tool for undoing nuts and bolts: ___ ___ ENCH
 b to twist the water out of wet clothes: ___ ___ ING
 c not right: W ___ ___ ___ G
 d to make marks on paper: ___ ___ ___ TE
 e to move like a worm: W ___ ___ GGLE

6 **Draw a line** to match these **either/or** pairs.

a black **or**	full
b wet **or**	going
c sunny **or**	white
d coming **or**	dry
e empty **or**	cloudy

Grammar

Adjectives stand in **front of nouns**.

Example There was a young (adjective) lady (noun) from Ryde.

Adjectives can also **follow verbs**.

Example Ivan's tongue turned (verb) green (adjective) when he ate licorice.

Adjectives tell us **size**, **shape**, **colour** and **number**.

Examples big, square, red, four

Adjectives can also tell us **mood**, **personality** and **special features**.

Examples happy, mean, heavy

1 **Circle** all the adjectives of colour and shape in these sentences.

a Clowns are often tall and thin, have red noses and wear baggy pants.

b Laurel was a skinny comedian who walked with bandy legs. Hardy, his partner, had the build of a round ball with two little feet under it and a round black hat on top.

2 **Circle** all the adjectives of mood and personality.

a Harry invited the lonely newcomer to join his jolly group of friends.

b Selfish people are never happy people.

c Mrs Georgiou is a thoughtful woman. She is kind to everyone.

3 **Circle** all the adjectives that tell us about special features.

a Planets are visible but many stars are invisible to the naked eye.

b These apples are ripe but the oranges are unripe.

c Taipans are venomous snakes but green tree snakes are harmless.

Punctuation

Sometimes we **abbreviate** (shorten) words. We call these shortened words **contractions**.

When we abbreviate we insert an apostrophe (') in place of the missing letter or syllable.

Example This **is not** my hat. → This **isn't** my hat.

Abbreviate the underlined words and **insert** an apostrophe in place of the missing letters.

1 He is not a good comedian. People do not laugh at his jokes.

______________________ ______________________

2 I have not laughed so much in a long time. She is a great comedian.

______________________ ______________________

Fun with words

1 English is a funny language. Can you **complete** these sayings?

a If something makes me laugh I say it T __ CKL __ S my fancy.
b If I hit my elbow and squeal with pain I wail that I hit my F __ NN __ bone.
c If I laugh till I cry I say I laughed my H __ __ D off.
d If I feel dizzy I say my head is SPI __ __ ING.

Lots of fun can be had by making up words. Lewis Carroll once wrote a poem called *The Jabberwocky*. Two of its lines are:

'Twas brillig and the slithy toves
did gyre and gimble in the wabe.

Most of these words are inventions but somehow they seem to make sense because we recognise nouns and adjectives and verbs among them.

2 Can you **answer** these questions?

a What were the ***toves*** doing? ____________ ing and ____________ ing (verbs)
b Where were they doing this? In the ________________ (noun)
c What was the weather like? It was ________________. (adjective)
d What were the ***toves*** like? They were ________________. (adjective)

3 Now it is your turn. **Invent** words to name the following:

a **One noun** to name a small furry animal shaped like a ball with no arms or legs and only one eye: ____________________
b **Two verbs** for the actions of this animal: __________________ __________________
c **One adjective** to describe the animal: ________________
d **One adjective** to describe the hot sticky weather: ________________
e **One noun** to name the green rain that is falling: ________________

4 Using your new words, **complete** this sentence. Your new sentence will follow the pattern of *The Jabberwocky* sentence above.

'Twas ____________________ and the ____________________ ____________________

did ____________________ and ____________________ in the ____________________.

Ask your friends what they see when you read them your sentence. You will be surprised.

5 These people all make their living out of being funny. Can you **name** them?

a __ __ __ __ __N b M __ __ __ __ __ __ __ __ __ c V __ __ T __ __ L __ Q __ __ __ __ __

Your turn to write

Tip for top writers

When you write a limerick, **check** its rhythm by **reading it aloud**. If the rhythm is regular it will sound like this: *de da / de da / de da / de da*

Example There was / a young / lady / from Ryde
de da / de da / deda / de da

1 Can you **complete** the second line of this introduction to a limerick with a **rhyming** word?
There was an old man from Coonamble
Who loved to wander and R __ M __ LE

2 Here are some limerick first lines. Can you **add** their second lines from the box below?

a There once was a lady from Niger ______________________

b There once was a miner called Pyner ______________________

c There was an old man from Japan ______________________

Who sported an awful black shiner
Who only ate water with bran
Who went for a ride on a tiger

3 Here are some first lines for limericks. Can you **write** a second line for each one? Remember that the last words of each line must rhyme. The first is done for you.

a There was an old man in the **hills**
Who swallowed so many green **pills**

b There once was a witch with a cat
____

c There once was a painter named Jim
____

d There was a green frog in a bog
____

4 Now that you have the idea, **choose** one of the first lines above (or make up one of your own) and **write** a limerick. Remember to write no more than five lines.

____

____

____

____

____

Answers on page 72

Chapter 4 Writing an information report

We write a **report** to **inform** our reader. It is a **factual**, not an imaginative piece of writing.

STRUCTURE

LANGUAGE

Bees

Introduction statement followed by explanation

Bees are very strange creatures. They have their own way of telling each other that they have found a new flower. They bring some of its nectar back to the hive and then do a little dance that shows where the flower is and how far away it is.

Adjective introduces idea of bees being interesting

Body of report (in groups of facts)

Autumn work

In autumn the worker bees go out and collect as much nectar and pollen as they can carry. Then they return to make honey and store it for the long cold winter.

Technical words

Hives

Bees build hives but they are not always dome-shaped like people draw them in storybooks. They are usually five storeys high. The queen bee always has the bottom storey. In between the bottom storey and all the rest there are bars only just wide enough for the workers to squeeze through. The queen bee can never go up to the other floors because she is bigger than all the other bees.

Short factual statements

Chambers and workers

The storeys the queen can't enter are where the store chambers are. There are chambers for pollen and nectar and royal jelly. If there is a fire the workers have to seal the walls and entrance of the chambers. They have to move the honey and the nectar and pollen away from the hot walls of the chamber.

Clear informative verbs

Queens and drones

The queen bee is the only bee that can lay eggs. She mates with a male bee called a drone. Once the queen has laid the eggs she throws the drone out because a drone just sits around eating honey and nectar. He cannot go out and collect pollen because drones do not have pollen-carrying sacs on their legs like the workers have.

Technical words

Young bees and growing up

Young bees are called nurses because they have to nurse the newborn bees whether they like it or not. What a bee ends up being when it grows up depends on what it eats. If it is to be a queen it must feed on royal jellies and it must never, ever set eyes on another queen. If it does they must fight till only one of them is still alive.

Only absolutely necessary adjectives used in a report

Penny (aged 9)

What did you read?

1. **Circle** the correct answer.
Bees communicate the location of a new hive by **action/sound**.

2. **Name** two activities that keep bees busy in autumn.

a ____

b ____

3. **Circle** the correct answer.
The queen bee occupies a chamber in the middle of the hive. **True/false**

4. **Explain** why the queen is unable to move between the floors of the hive.

____

5. **Circle** the correct answer.
Drones/Nurses are the bees that look after the newborn bees.

6. **Circle** the correct answer. A sac is a:
a small basket carried by bees
b tiny pocket on the legs of bees
c spelling mistake

7. **Complete** this sentence.
What a young bee grows up to be depends on ____________________

____

How is it written?

1. A report contains facts. **Name** two facts you find in paragraph three.

____

____

2. A report uses technical words. **Write** down three technical words you find in the report.

________________ ________________ ________________

3. A report includes no opinions, only facts. It is usually written in the third person (he, she, it, they).
Circle the **two** sentences that would **not** appear in a report:
a I like insects.
b Insects come in all sizes and shapes.
c I think insects are funny.

4. **Complete** the following.
Adjectives in reports usually tell us SH ___PE, C ___LOUR, S ___ZE and N ___MB ___R.

Spelling and meaning

collect	storey	chamber	communicate
pollen	creature	entrance	strange
nectar	squeeze	laid	dome

Pay special attention to **double letters** and to **final syllables** when you are learning spelling and don't forget the **look**, **cover**, **write and check** method of learning to spell.

1 **Insert** a word from the word box.

a Birds ______________ straw and twigs to build their nests.
b ______________ is found at the centre of a flower.
c Humpback whales ______________ by singing to each other.
d ______________ to the zoo costs five dollars for children.
e An igloo is a ______________-shaped house built of ice.

Not all plurals (more then one) end in ***~s***. Some have different endings. Some are different words altogether and some words don't change at all.
Examples bee → bees, mouse → mice, sheep → sheep

2 **Write** the plural of each of the following creatures. Your dictionary will help.

a horse ______________ b fish ______________
c pig ______________ d cow ______________
e goose ______________ f koala ______________

3 **Write** the plurals of these nouns.

a creature ______________ b storey ______________
c burrow ______________ d hive ______________
e hatchery ______________ f hutch ______________

Words that sound the same but are spelt differently are called **homonyms**.
Example **story** (a narrative) and **storey** (one level in a tall building)

4 **Draw a line** from each homonym to the right meaning.

a bore	town leader
b boar	passenger boat
c mare	male pig
d mayor	female horse
e ferry	tiny invisible creature with wings
f fairy	source of underground water

Grammar

Careful choice of **verbs** is very important in a report. A verb is a word that tells us about **doing**, **being**, **saying**, **having and the use of all our senses**.

Examples Dingoes ***stalk*** injured animals. (doing verb)
All the bees ***are*** in the hive. (being verb)
Dogs ***hear*** sounds unheard by us (sense of hearing verb)

1 **Circle** all the verbs in these sentences:

a Peewits build cup-shaped nests of mud and straw.
b Snakes hibernate over winter.
c Ants are very intelligent insects.
d An eclipse of the sun is a rare event.
e Eagles watch the ground from high in the air.

2 Sometimes a verb contains more than one word (e.g. Fruit bats ***are hanging*** upside down in the mango tree). **Circle** the **complete verbs** in these sentences.

a Little brown geckoes were sunning themselves on a rock.
b A mob of kangaroos is resting in the shade.
c Three lions were hunting an antelope.
d A blue whale was cruising close to the ice pack.

3 **Complete** the sentences below by inserting a verb made from the underlined adjective in the sentence above. The first is done for you.

a Swallows are <u>migratory</u> birds.
Swallows **migrate** between China and Australia.
b Bears are <u>hibernating</u> animals.
Bears ___ ___ ___ ___ ___ ___ ___ ___ ___ in caves over winter.
c Cattle gather in <u>defensive</u> herds.
Cattle gather in herds to ___ ___ ___ ___ ___ ___ themselves.

Punctuation

When we write **lists** (of things or of activities) we **separate** the items in the list with a comma (**,**) except for the **last two items**, which are separated by the word ***and***.

Example Mountaineers can walk**,** climb**,** abseil**,** crawl ***and*** slide all in one day.

Insert all the missing commas:

a Ants stand guard hunt trap build climb and migrate.
b Pandas are only known for sleeping eating and sleeping again.
c Dolphins are famed for diving leaping out of the water barrelling and somersaulting.

Fun with words

1 Animal babies have special names (e.g. baby cows are calves). Can you **name** these animal babies? Your dictionary will help you.

a A baby bird is a NE __ __ LING.
b A baby elephant is a C A __ F.
c A baby lion is a C __ __.
d A baby fish is a FING __ __ LING.
e A baby whale is a C __ LF.
f A baby swan is a CYG __ __ T.

2 Some creatures are only **active at night**. We call them **nocturnal** creatures. **Find** all the nocturnal creatures in this cage and release them into the night by writing their names among the moon and stars.

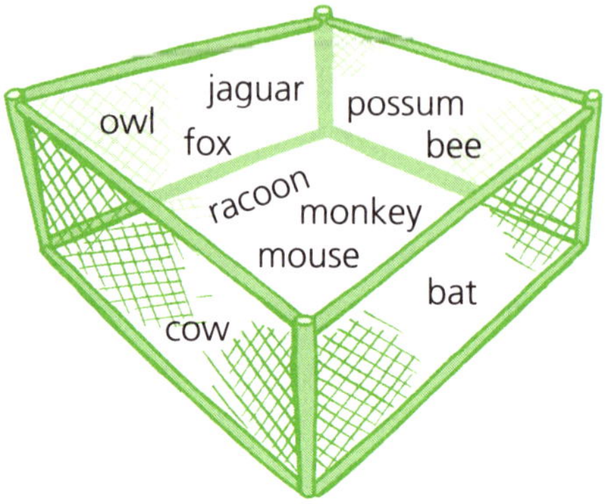

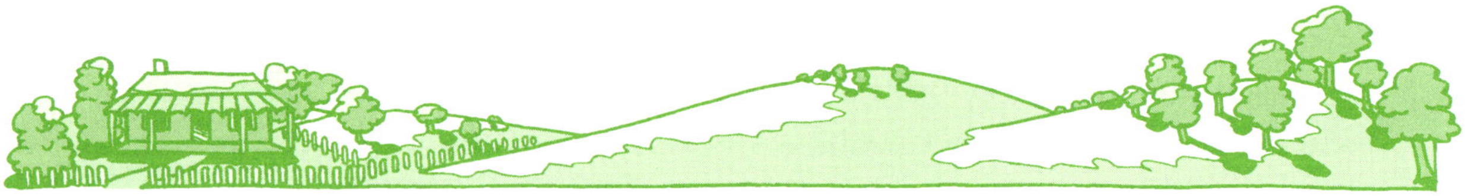

3 Most animal homes have a special name. With the help of your dictionary can you **name** these homes?

a an eagle's nest: EYR __ __
b a maze of connected rabbit burrows: WA __ R __ N
c a turkey's nest: MOU __ D
d a wild dog's hole or cave: LA __ R

Your turn to write

Tip for top writers

When you **write** a report make sure you:

- only write facts;
- choose precise verbs;
- use technical words where needed;
- use only factual adjectives.

Using the facts in the box, **write** a report on the giant anaconda on the scaffold provided.

- water snake
- found in tropical rivers (South America)
- so-called because of size: average length 5 metres and some longer
- heavily built
- dark green with large oval black spots
- hunts at night
- prey: small animals, birds, other reptiles
- lies in wait in water
- kills by constriction: wraps prey in coils and crushes it
- nests in leaf litter on jungle floor
- can produce up to 75 young at one time

THE GIANT ANACONDA

Identification and location ______________________________

____

____

Appearance ______________________________

____

____

____

Nest and young ______________________________

____

____

____

Prey ______________________________

____

Hunting habits ______________________________

____

____

____

Conclusion ______________________________

____

____

Answers on pages 72–73

Chapter 5 Writing a description of a place

Place descriptions usually occur inside a longer text (e.g. a narrative or a recount). When we **describe** a place we aim to make that place real to the reader.

STRUCTURE | LANGUAGE

Grandfather's old shed

Orientation

Down the back of Grandfather's place there is a very old wooden shed. It might have been painted green once but now it's mostly the grey wood goes when it is old with just a few peeling patches of green on the door.

Good detail

Body of description

Outside appearance

It has a crooked door and a crooked roof. Even its walls are crooked. It leans towards the fence as if it's been pushed. Maybe the wind pushed it for years and years till it just got tired of standing up straight.

Repetition emphasises age

The day I got to see inside the shed was wet. By mid-morning I had nothing to do. Grandfather, who doesn't like people standing around idle, gave me an umbrella and sent me down to the shed.

Good choice of adjective

"Have a look around and see if you can find me a long weight," he told me with a wink. "It might take you a while."

First impressions

I ran down to the shed happily, pushed the door open and sneezed. Dust fell all over me. There was dust everywhere. Cobwebs hung in corners and around the shelves that lined the walls. It was dark and very dusty but it smelled nice: a bit like sunshine and grease and chopped wood all mixed together.

Details of sight and smell

The floor

Odd lengths of timber, some pieces of guttering and a wooden ladder lay across the rafters over my head. There was nothing like a long weight up there. I began to turn through the boxes stacked up on the floor among wood shavings from long ago. Some held old-fashioned tools and pieces of coiled wire, others held dusty old bottles that I think were preserving jars and one box was full of really old Donald Duck comics. I told myself I would come back here later and read them all.

Interesting details

The shelves

I stood up and looked along the shelves. There were two funny old lamps with glass tops and round metal tanks with wicks in them. Further on I found a row of bottles in all sorts of shapes and sizes and they were all blue.

Place words to make different position clear

Blue glass was something I had not seen before. I took one of the bottles over to the window to look at it properly. When I rubbed the dust off it and held it up to the light the sun suddenly came out. Shining through the bottle glass it threw a lovely blue light over my hands.

Conclusion

When I went back to the house I told Grandfather I couldn't find a long weight but that I'd found this beautiful blue bottle. He laughed and washed the bottle for me, saying I could keep it.

Comment

Then he said, "There are two ways of spelling 'weight', you know." I am still thinking about that one.

Joke — a homonym joke

What did you read?

1 **Circle** the correct answer. The shed is made of:

a corrugated iron   b fibro   c wood

2 **Circle** the correct answer. The shed is crooked because:

a it's old   b perhaps the wind pushed it

c it was built that way

3 When the writer entered the shed **what two things** immediately confirmed that it was very old?

a ______________________   b ______________________

4 **Why** did the writer like the smell of the shed?

____

5 **What** is the other spelling of ***weight***? ______________________

6 Why did the writer's grandfather really send him to the shed?

____

____

How is it written?

1 **Circle** the most correct answer. Where do we read about the shed first?

a in the first paragraph   b in the first sentence

c in the fourth paragraph

2 The writer used his sense of sight to show us what he saw in the shed. What other senses did he use? **Circle** all the correct answers.

a taste   b touch

c smell   d hearing

3 **Circle** the correct answer. When describing the interior of the shed the writer mentioned:

a the structure of the shed (floor, walls, window and rafters)

b the contents of the shed

c both of the above

4 **Circle** two correct answers. The writer describes the contents of the shed because:

a they are part of what is fascinating about the shed

b there's not much you can write about an old shed

c they explain what the shed is used for

5 **Complete** this sentence.

A place description requires the careful choice of ADJ ___ ___ T ___ VES.

Spelling and meaning

crooked	weight	label	towards
straight	wait	laugh	idle
umbrella	grease	wooden	sneeze

When you spell, say the word aloud and clearly. Then learn to spell it. Many people have trouble spelling ***umbrella*** because they do not say it correctly. It only has three syllables ***um/brell/a***.

1 **Insert** a word from the box in the blanks.

a Please draw a ____________ line margin down the page.
b The carrier struggled under the ____________ of his load.
c The ____________ on the bottle warned, Poison! Dangerous!
d All the traffic stood ____________ while police removed the wrecked vehicles.
e People cough and ____________ with the common cold.

2 There is **one word** in the word box that can be used as both a **verb** and a **noun**. **Find** it and **insert** it in this sentence.

Please __ __ __ __ __ __ the hinges on the shed door to stop it squeaking but don't get

__ __ __ __ __ __ on your jeans.

3 **Choose** the correct homonym from the box below to insert in the following sentences.

wait	reeds	pale	peel	reel	weight	reads	pail	peal	real

a Cold driving rain and a bitter wind made the long __ __ __ __ seem endless.
b A __ __ __ __ of bells drifted across the valley in the stillness of the evening.
c The only sound was the rustle of ducks among the __ __ __ __ __ beside the river.
d Beside the tackle box stood a brand new rod and __ __ __ __.
e In the corner of the shed stood a battered old dairy __ __ __ __ for carrying milk.
f Among the coins in the dusty chest was a __ __ __ __ old English gold sovereign.
g The faded paint on the old fence was beginning to __ __ __ __.

4 Words that mean the opposite are called **antonyms**. **Draw a line** from the antonyms in column B to the words in column A.

A	B
a straight	busy
b laugh	open
c idle	crooked
d build	cry
e close	demolish

Grammar

Compound sentences have two equally important parts. Each contains a verb and both parts are joined by ***and***, ***but*** or ***or***.

Examples Julie will play (verb) the flute ***and*** Wafa will play (verb) the saxophone.
Kang will play (verb) the drums ***or*** he will play (verb) violin at the eisteddford.

Complex sentences have **one important part** (principal clause) and **one less important part** (subordinate clause). Both parts contain verbs and both parts are joined by a joining word (conjunction). In this example the subordinate clause is underlined.

Example The house **is** (verb) in good condition ***although*** (joining word) its roof **needs** (verb) paint.

1. **Name** these sentences **compound** or **complex** in the space provided.
   - a If you have too many boxes you can store them in our garage. ______________
   - b We store paint in the shed and we store timber across its rafters. ______________
   - c John can clean the shelves or help Peter wash the windows. ______________
   - d Because the house is derelict it will be demolished. ______________

2. **Underline** all the principal clauses and **circle** all the subordinate clauses.
   - a Unless there is a breeze the paint won't dry.
   - b While we were in the old shed we saw a redback spider.
   - c Even though there were cobwebs in the attic we were not frightened.

3. **Make** one sentence out of each of these sentence pairs by using joining words such as ***though***, ***although***, ***if***, ***unless***, ***while***, ***when***. The joining word may start the sentence.
   - a It is raining. I will go to the bakery. ______________________________
   - b It is so old. The school still has not fallen down. ______________________________
   - c You are here. We will paint the fence. ______________________________

Punctuation

Inverted commas (**"~"**) enclose the exact words someone says.

Example **"**Have a look around and see if you can find me a long weight,**"** he said.

1. **Insert** all necessary inverted commas.
   - a Does dust make you sneeze? Ibrahim asked Paul.
   - b Hand me some more nails, the carpenter told his apprentice.

If the actual words spoken are broken by other words, **enclose only the words spoken in inverted commas**.

Example **"**I've dropped these,**"** he sighed, **"**pass me some more screws, please.**"**

2. **Insert** all necessary inverted commas.
   - a Help! he shouted. The wind is lifting the roof off!
   - b I know you like the beach, said Melissa, but I prefer the mountains.

Fun with words

1 In his grandfather's shed our writer found all sorts of things. Here they are in scrambled form. Can you **unscramble** them? You have a clue in the first letter.

a TTOBLES B____________ b MOCCIS C____________

c SPLAM L____________ d LOOTS T____________

2 The following are all words naming buildings. **Choose** the correct one for each illustration.

observatory	skyscraper	cottage	cathedral	igloo	lighthouse	mosque

a ____________

b ____________

c ____________

d ____________

3 People have used hand tools for many years. Can you **name** the hand tools for these tasks?

a fixing nails: H ___ ___ M ___ R

b cutting building timber: S ___ ___

c fixing screws: S___ ___ ___ ___ DR ___ ___ ___ R

d fixing nuts and bolts: SP ___ ___ N ___ R

e carving wood: CH ___ S ___ L

4 **Follow** these instructions.

a **Cut** a length of string two metres twenty-five centimetres long.

b Use the top 10 centimetres to **tie** the string to the **middle** of a pencil.

c **Tie** a knot in the string every 50 centimetres down from the pencil.

d Use the 15 or so centimetres left to **tie** to a small heavy weight (e.g. a small egg cup, a small piece of heavy wood or a small stone, even a small heap of sand wrapped in cling-plastic).

e Now you have made a measuring tool. You can use it to **measure** how deep something is or how high it is. **Hold** the pencil level and just drop the bob (the weight) to the bottom of what you want to measure. When the string is still, count the knots in the string to the top of what you are measuring. Then you multiply the number of knots by 50 centimetres and you have your measurement.

5 To name the tool you have just made **answer** the questions below.

a Small stone fruit with dark red skin ___ ___ ___ ___

b Short for 'Robert' ___ ___ ___

This tool, used for thousands of years, is called a ___ ___ ___ ___ B ___ ___ ___

Your turn to write

Tip for top writers

When describing a place first **tell** where it is and then **tell** all about it, including what you **see**, **hear**, **smell**, **feel** and **think** about it.

1 Stand in the doorway of your kitchen and **look** at it carefully. **Ask** these questions.

a Where is the kitchen in my house?

b What happens in this kitchen? (Don't just think about cooking.)

c How is it laid out? What is the busiest part? Why is that so?

d Who uses this kitchen?

e Is it more or less important than other parts of the house? Why?

f What can I see and what can I smell in this kitchen?

g Is it always the same?

h Is there anything I really like or dislike in this kitchen? (Think about colours, sounds, smells, shapes, chores, routines and so on.)

2 Using the answers to your questions, write a description of the kitchen in your house.

Orientation ______________________________

____

____

Paragraph 1 *(What happens in the kitchen)* ______________________________

____

____

Paragraph 2 *(People in the kitchen)* ______________________________

____

____

Paragraph 3 *(What's special about our kitchen)* ______________________________

____

____

____

Comment *(What I think/feel about our kitchen)* ______________________________

____

Answers on pages 73–74

Chapter 6 Expressing your opinion in a speech (exposition)

An **opinion speech** states an argument, argues it strongly and concludes by restating the argument and inviting the audience to agree.

STRUCTURE | LANGUAGE

Television's negative influence

Address (to audience)

Good morning, Year Four,

Statement of argument

I believe television influences our community in a negative way. Television influences people to copy what they see. Programs and advertising both influence people to copy what they see. They buy products because they saw them on TV. They talk and act the way the characters on their favourite shows do. This is definitely a case of TV having a negative influence on people.

All definite statements (no "I think")

Body of case (evidence to support argument)

TV advertisements influence the way people buy things. Advertisements intrigue them with their bright colours and loud music. Advertisers only tell you good things about a product and not the bad things so people are persuaded to buy things they don't need. Sometimes they buy worthless things or things that break. Television advertising encourages people to waste money.

Good choice of verbs

When people watch the same show on TV a number of times they start to pick up the habits of characters on the show. Some of these habits are extremely bad, like laziness, bad attitudes and even swearing and hurting.

Examples explain statement

Children see lots of violence on TV, real violence and cartoon violence. A survey carried out by the International Coalition Against Violence showed that many cartoons are violent. "Bugs Bunny" and "Road Runner" show an average of fifty-five violent acts every hour. The News every night is full of violence too. That is worse because it's real violence and in cartoons it's just pretend.

Quotations from authorities make your case believable

Dr Patricia Edgar, Director of the Australian Children's Television Foundation, says, "Children are more afraid of what they see on the News than on other shows because they know it is real". I think she is right and this is not good for children. Television should not show violence to frighten us. Children need to learn to be friends. We should not learn about violence.

Statements everyone can agree with to win approval of audience

Conclusion

Television definitely has a very negative influence on our community. We should all be very worried about it.

Audience included in statement

Stephanie (aged 9)

What did you read?

1. **Who** is the audience listening to this speech? ____________________

2. **What** is it that catches people's attention about advertisements?

   a ____________________ b ____________________

3. **Name** two bad habits the speaker believes TV watchers can pick up.

   a ____________________ b ____________________

4. **Circle** the correct answer.
   Dr Patricia Edgar is the Director of the International Coalition Against Violence. **True/False?**

5. The speaker considers TV a negative influence for several reasons. **Circle** the reason she **does not** mention.
   a People copy bad habits.
   b People buy worthless things.
   c People waste money on things they don't need.
   d There are too many crime shows on TV.
   e There is a lot of violence on TV.

How is it written?

1. **What** words in the first sentence tell us that this is an **opinion** speech? ____________________

2. **Circle** the most correct answer. The writer's opinion first appears in:
   a the first paragraph b the first line c the last line

3. **Circle** the correct answer. The writer's opinion is restated in:
   a the middle of the speech b the last paragraph c the second-last paragraph

4. To persuade others to share your opinion it helps to include facts to support what you say. **Write** down one fact you find in paragraph four.

   ____

   ____

5. An opinion is always more believable if supported by someone in authority. This speaker quotes two authorities. **Name** one of them.

   ____

6. When persuading an audience to agree with your opinion it is helpful to include them in your speech. **Circle** the words below that **include** the audience (they are all in the last two paragraphs).

   a us b violence c our d influence e we

Spelling and meaning

television	**positive**	**extremely**	**waste**
influence	**negative**	**attitude**	**money**
community	**advertisement**	**international**	**product**

Sometimes it helps to recognise the meaning of **prefixes** (first syllables) when you are learning to spell (e.g. the prefix ***tele~***, which means *far* or *at a distance*, and the prefix ***inter~***, which means *between*). Then you only have to learn the rest of the word.

1 Remembering that the prefix ***inter~*** means *between*, **match** these words to their meanings.

a interrupt		between states
b international		come between two quarrelling people
c interstate		get in the way of someone and their work
d intersection		between countries
e intervene		point where two roads meet
f interfere		break into a conversation

2 **Label** these pictures with a ***tele~*** word.

a ____________ b ____________ c ____________ pole

3 **Insert** a word from the word box to complete these sentences.

a Our street is a little ____________ of friends and neighbours.

b Rain will have a bad ____________ on the way a horse gallops.

c The positive effect of rain is garden growth, the ____________ effect is the cancellation of our picnic.

d It is ____________ cold in Ottawa today at minus 8 degrees Celsius.

e The Olympic Games is an ____________ sports gathering.

Grammar

Adverbs tell us things about a verb. They tell us **how**, **when** and **where** an action happens.

Examples Regina reads well. (adverb, how)
Omar was sick yesterday. (adverb, when)
The cat sleeps there. (adverb, where)

Adverbs also tell us about adjectives. They tell us to what **degree** the adjective is true.

Examples I am very excited about going on holidays.
Peter only injured himself slightly when he fell.

Many adverbs end in ***~ly***.

Examples finally, hungrily, usually, rarely

1 **Circle** the **adverbs** in these sentences.

a Television advertisements for toys are shown early in the day.
b Jodie watches nature programs eagerly.
c Digital television is usually very expensive.
d Game shows are common on television because they can be made cheaply.
e Young viewers react positively to comedies and cartoons.

2 **Circle** the **adverbs** in these sentences and **write *how***, ***when*** or ***where*** in the space provided to show what the adverb tells us.

a Mr Sung is advertising a sale today. ______________________
b News reports usually occur between 6 and 7 pm. ______________________
c Television cameras are fixed on the finishing line over there. ______________________
d Australia's *Playschool* is watched internationally. ______________________
e Some advertising influences people negatively. ______________________

Punctuation

All writing is arranged in **paragraphs**: **one idea** per paragraph, **one event** per paragraph, **one speaker** per paragraph.

Read the following opinion carefully and then **mark** where each new paragraph should begin with a **square bracket** (**[**).

I firmly believe that if you have a pet you should look after it as if it is a member of your family. After all, it lives in the same house as you and shares every part of your life, probably even more closely than your friends do. So what does looking after your pet like family mean? First, it means your pet is fed daily. It means it is fed what is right for its breed, not just scraps from the kitchen. It means you make sure it has plenty of clean fresh water to drink every day. Like us, pets feel the heat and the cold. In winter you must make sure it has a warm dry shelter out of the wind and rain and in summer you must see that it has lots of cool shade to protect it from the heat. If it is sick you take it to the vet and if it is miserable you play with it and reassure it that it is your friend. We owe our pets the same loyal friendship they give us.

Fun with words

1 Television screens many different kinds of programs. Here are the names of some of them. Can you **match** the word to the program it names?

a animation		competition with competitors and prizes
b drama		how to improve your life, house, garden, holidays
c current affairs		story in cartoon format
d lifestyle		serious, acted story about people and events
e comedy		program discussing real events and issues
f game show		program designed to make you laugh

2 Communities are groups of living creatures who live together. Below are names of human communities. **Number** them in order from smallest to largest.

metropolis   city   village   town

3 These people are all happy, but some are happier than others. Using the adverbs ***very***, ***rather*** and ***extremely*** **label** them according to their degree of happiness.

We are the Happy Family

a ____________ b ____________ c ____________

4 When you give a speech you must first **address** your audience. **Match** these terms of address to their audiences.

a Ladies and Gentlemen		a judge
b Your Excellency		a minister named Smith
c Fellow Footballers		mixed adults
d Your Honour		an ambassador
e Reverend Smith		your football team

Your turn to write

Tip for top writers

In an opinion speech:

- **Start** with an address/greeting to the audience.
- **State** your opinion.
- **Explain** and argue your opinion.
- **Use** facts and quotations to **support** your opinion.
- **End** by restating your opinion and asking the audience to agree.

1. **Make a list** of the arguments you could use to support the opinion that everyone should play a sport.

   a ____

   ____

   b ____

   ____

   c ____

   ____

   d ____

   ____

2. **Write a statement of opinion** to introduce the arguments you have written in question 1.

   ____

   ____

   ____

   ____

   ____

3. Re-read your answers to questions 1 and 2 and then **write a conclusion** to this expression of your opinion.

   ____

   ____

   ____

Answers on pages 74–75

Chapter 7 Writing an explanation of what happens

Explaining what happens is a special kind of writing. It is always written in the **present tense** and it is always **factual**. Make sure of your facts by doing some **research** before writing an explanation.

STRUCTURE

LANGUAGE

Drought and dust

Introduction short, factual

When long rainless years have burned away all the grass and turned the land to dust only wind is needed to create a dust storm.

One sentence includes everything necessary to make a dust storm

Body of explanation Dust movement

A dust storm is a moving wall of dust. Strong winds sweeping over bare land lift the dust into the air and carry it away, sometimes thousands of kilometres away. Dust storms from south-eastern Australia have travelled right across the Tasman Sea, producing dust-coloured "red snow" on the New Zealand Alps.

Definition

Place names make distance statement believable

Effects of dust

During a dust storm the air is so thick with dust that visibility is reduced to a few paces. One side of a street becomes invisible to the other. Dust clogs breathing, stings eyes and finds its way inside clothing. It gets into houses, cupboards, clothes in drawers, even inside the pages of books. It blocks up air conditioners and fouls car radiators. It gets into the workings of fine machinery and damages their parts.

Big to small detail tells us how fine dust is

Dust and rain

If a dust storm travels far enough to run into a rain storm the rain that reaches the ground will leave mud streaks down the sides of buildings, ruin washing lines of laundry and leave muddy puddles on concrete.

Worst effect

The worst effect of the combination of drought and wind to produce a dust storm is the loss of topsoil. This is the top level of soil containing all the nutrients that plants need to grow. When it is picked up and blown away by the wind crops struggle to survive in the poor soils that are left.

Technical words

Good, clear verb

Conclusion

Drought and the resulting dust storms are one of the greatest threats to the Australian environment.

What did you read?

1. Drought makes a dust storm possible. **Circle** the answer that actually **starts** a dust storm.
   a farmers b wind c lack of rain d bare ground

2. **Circle** the correct answer. Dust storms from Australia have been known to cross the:
   a Tasman Sea b Coral Sea c Timor Sea

3. **Circle** the correct answer. When a dust storm meets a rain storm:
   a the rain dries up b the dust storm stops
   c the rain is turned to muddy water

4. **List** two ways in which dust storms affect people personally.
   a ____________________
   b ____________________

5. **How** does dust affect fine machinery?
   ____
   ____

6. **Explain** why crops would struggle to survive in the year following a dust storm.
   ____
   ____

How is it written?

1. **Circle** the correct answer.
   We learn what causes a dust storm in the first paragraph. **True/False**

2. A good explanation includes a definition. **Write** the definition of a dust storm used in this text.
   ____

3. **What fact** does the writer include to prove that dust storms can travel far?
   ____

4. **Complete** this statement.
   The writer shows how dust can get into tiny spaces by listing spaces from L ___ ___ GEST to SM ___ ___ ___ EST.

5. **Complete** this sentence.
   The explanation ends with an emphasis on how serious a PR ___ B ___ ___ M a dust storm really is.

Spelling and meaning

drought	visible	move	travel
create	visibility	moving	travelled
colour	sometimes	bare	traveller

Verbs that end in **e**, drop the **e** when you add ***ing*** (e.g. move/moving).
Verbs that end in ***l***, double that ***l*** when you add **any suffix** (end syllable) (e.g. travel/traveller).

1 **Insert** the correct form of the word in brackets.

a The camel train was ________________ (travel) towards an oasis.
b We are ________________ (move) to Jakarta for two years.
c This experiment is ________________ (prove) that water is made of oxygen and hydrogen.
d My brother is ________________ (label) his cricket gear.
e We are still ________________ (decide) whether to go to the movies.

2 **Match** these words from the word box to their meaning.

a drought		make
b create		occasionally
c sometimes		without covering
d bare		a long time without rain

3 Sometimes we can make **antonyms** (words that mean the opposite) by adding a **prefix** (beginning syllable). **Make** antonyms of these words by adding the prefix ***in~***.

a visible (able to be seen) ________________________

b audible (able to be heard) ________________________

c tangible (able to be touched) ________________________

4 **Substitute** one word for the phrase in brackets.

a In all the noise of the wind and thunder the ring of the telephone was ________________________ (could not be heard).

b The mountain top was ________________________ (could not be seen) because of the low cloud.

c The scent of flowers is an ________________________ (cannot be touched) delight.

5 Some common homonyms (same sound, different spelling) can cause confusion. **Finish labelling** these pictures correctly.

a

b

c

d

a Please don't ______________ on the wall.

b Please shut the ______________.

c There's a ______________ in there.

d The cupboard was ______________.

Grammar—Adverb revision

1 **Circle** the adverbs of degree in these sentences.
- a He was absolutely amazed at his first sight of the dust storm.
- b I know all about cyclones but I am less certain about dust storms.
- c Sue is very confident of completing her weather project on time.

2 **Circle** all the adverbs of time, place, degree and manner (how) in the following sentences.
- a The kite danced wildly at the end of its string in the high wind.
- b Tomorrow we will go on our excursion to the weather bureau.
- c Keisha was very frightened when the dust made it hard to breathe.

Punctuation

We already know an **apostrophe** (**'**) shows us where a letter has been left out (e.g. is not → isn't, has not → hasn't).
An apostrophe also shows us that **someone owns something** (e.g. Wiki's football boots, Selena**'s** hockey stick).

1 **Insert** an apostrophe where necessary.
- a A farmers worst nightmare is a dust storm during a drought.
- b A plants survival depends on good topsoil and good rainfall.
- c Indias and Australias common problem is frequent drought.
- d A meteorologists job is to forecast weather patterns.

If a plural noun (more than one) owns something, the apostrophe is placed **after** the final ***s*** of that noun.
Example All the local farmer**s'** topsoil was swept away by the winds.
If the plural word does not end in ***s*** then the apostrophe comes at the end of the word.
Example The children**'s** shoes were all wet from the rain.

2 **Insert** an apostrophe where necessary.
- a High winds can damage birds wing feathers.
- b Horses hooves can be badly cracked by dry stony ground.
- c Farmers crops need plenty of water and sunlight.

Fun with words

1 These are all words meaning **dry**. Can you **unscramble** them?

a IDAR → A ___ ___ D

b RRENBA → B ___ R ___ ___ N

c STYDU → D ___ ___ TY

d THRIYST → T ___ ___ ___ STY

2 This paddock has been in drought for two years. **Fill** it up with all the words you can think of that are related to **drought**. Think about temperature, about plants, about animals, about the soil, about dams. One word has been put in already.

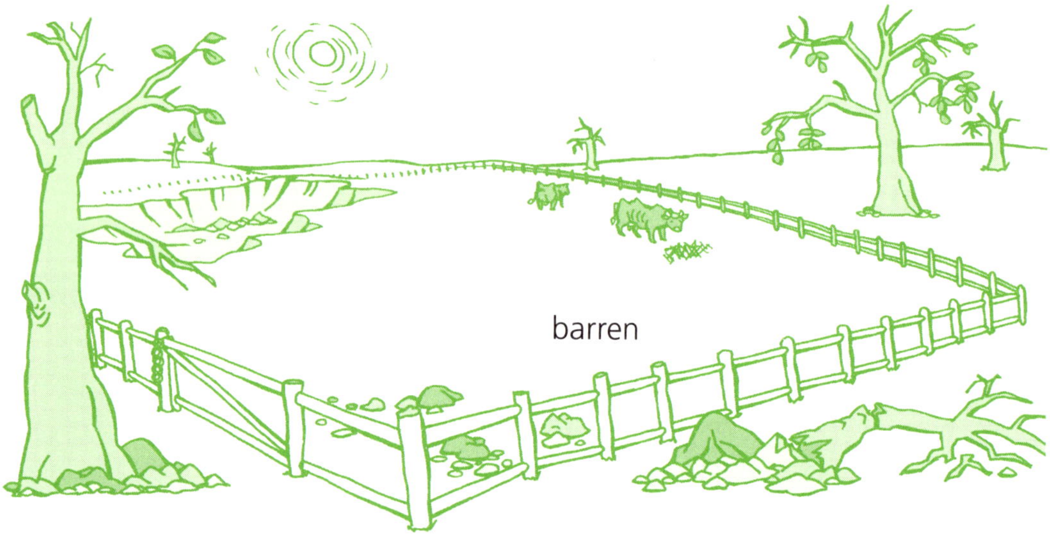

3 The most waterless areas of the world are called deserts. The things below are all found in deserts. Do you **know** what they are?

a four-legged animal sometimes called the ship of the desert: C ___ ___ ___ L

b tiny green place in the desert with water and palm trees: O ___ S ___ S

c small brown fruit of the desert palm tree: D ___ T ___

4 Dust storms are one kind of storm. There are many other kinds of storms. Can you **name** them?

a ___ ___ ___ ___ ___ CANE (think of moving faster so you won't be late)

b ___ ___ ___ ___ ONE (think of a bicycle losing some letters)

c ___ ___ ___ ___ ADO (think of a word meaning ***ripped***)

d ___ ___ ___ ___ (think of a homonym for ***Gail***)

e TYP ___ ___ ___ ___ (think of a slang word for showing off by driving too fast)

f TH ___ ___ ___ ___ ___ STORM (think of what goes with lightning)

Your turn to write

Tip for top writers

When explaining how things happen, first **research** your subject. Then:

- **start** with the cause;
- **explain** the consequences (results);
- **arrange** consequences in order of happening or of importance.

1 Sometimes we need to do some research before we write an explanation to make sure we have our facts right.

a **Choose** one of these subjects: Floods Fires Electricity blackouts

b Find out all you can about the subject by researching in books and encyclopaedias. You can also use the Internet and CD-ROMs in your school library.

2 **Write** an **introduction** that explains what causes your subject to happen.

3 **Write** a **list** of what happens in sequence.

1.

2.

3.

4.

5.

6.

4 **Write a conclusion** to what happens in your event by writing about its **long-term** consequences.

Example It can take up to thirty years to rebuild a city destroyed by an **earthquake**. Houses, shops and factories have to be rebuilt. Roads and bridges must be built. Water and power supplies must be restored and sewerage systems rebuilt.

5 Using your answers to all the questions so far, **write an explanation** of what happens in your event on your own paper. Make sure you put the edited explanation in your folder.

Answers on pages 75–76

Chapter 8 Writing pros and cons (discussion)

Pros and cons are points **for and against** an idea we are discussing. They are usually written in single sentences in order of importance, followed by a conclusion.

STRUCTURE

LANGUAGE

Should children always wear sunscreen?

Topic is usually a question to be answered

Pros (For)

Positive points in order of importance

1. Children should wear sunscreen all the time because without it we will get cancer when we are older.
2. If we wear sunscreen continually we won't get sunburned because the sunscreen protects our skin.
3. If we wear sunscreen all the time we will keep our own natural colour that we were born with and we won't get freckles.

One point per number

Cons (Against)

Negative points in order of importance

1. There's no point wearing sunscreen when we're asleep or when it is raining.
2. People already wear hats to protect them so they don't need to wear sunscreen too.
3. Some people actually like to have suntanned skin and sunscreen stops their skin from tanning.

Reasons make argument believable

Conclusion

Decision — (Pros win with some influence of cons)

We should wear sunscreen all the time **we are outside**. Even when it is a grey day we can still get sunburned. We will keep our own natural skin colour and we will not get skin cancer.

Pro argument with influence of con argument

Anthea (aged 8)

What did you read?

1. **Circle** the correct answer. This discussion is about:
   a skin colour b sunburn c wearing sunscreen

2. **Complete** this sentence. The most serious effect of going without sunscreen protection is

   ____

3. **Circle** the correct answer. When the writer refers to ***natural colouring*** she is referring to:
   a skin and hair colour b clothing colour c favourite colour

4. The writer says sunscreen protects us from sunburn. Do you know what sunburn is? **Explain** in one **complete sentence**.

   ____

   ____

5. There no point in wearing sunscreen while you are asleep in bed. Do you think this is a sensible point to make or a silly point?

   ____

6. **Think carefully** and **circle** the correct answer. Hats protect us against sunburn by:
   a keeping our heads cool
   b keeping the sun's rays from our face and ears
   c keeping rain off our hair

7. The con case influenced the conclusion of this discussion. **What words** in the **first** sentence of the conclusion tell us this?

   ____

How is it written?

1. **Circle** the correct word.
   The first pro and the first con points are the **strongest/weakest** arguments of each case.

2. **Complete** this sentence.
   Pro points are always F ___ ___ the idea being discussed and con points are always A ___ ___ ___ ___ ___ ___ that idea.

3. **Complete** this sentence. Points are always listed in order from ST ___ ___ ___ ___ EST to W ___ ___ ___ EST.

4. **Circle** the correct answer. Each point on this text is written as:
   a one sentence b one phrase

5. **Circle** the correct answer.
   The conclusion **can/cannot** be influenced by the arguments of the losing case.

Spelling and meaning

sunscreen	likely	wear	discussion
cancer	continually	protect	argument
sunburn	colouring	protection	conclusion

Sometimes letters represent more than one sound (e.g. the letter ***c***).
C can be a hard sound as in ***c****at* and a soft sound as in *ni****c****e*. These can be tricky and need careful practice.

1 a **Write** down three words in the word box that contain a **hard *c***.

________________ ________________ ________________

b The word ***cancer*** contains a hard ***c*** and a soft ***c***. **Circle** the **soft *c***. CANCER

2 The letter c is usually a **soft *c*** if it is followed by the letter ***e*** (e.g. lettu**ce**, re**ce**ive).
Write HARD or SOFT to describe the sound made by ***c*** in each of these words.

a cell ________________

b cellophane ________________

c cake ________________

d recipe ________________

e decent ________________

f decay ________________

3 **Insert** a word from the word box in the spaces.

a People who work outdoors are more ______________ to be sunburned than people who work indoors.

b Raincoats and gumboots ________________ us from the rain.

c It rained _______________________ overnight so the picnic was cancelled.

d It is sensible to ________________ hats in summertime.

e Without sunscreen Australians and New Zealanders are at high risk of getting skin

________________.

4 **Label** these pictures with a word from the word box.

a ____________________

b ____________________

c ____________________

Grammar

Verbs do very important things in sentences. They tell us what **is** and what **happens**. They can also tell us **when** it is and **when** it happens.

We call this time-telling **tense**. If we want to change the time (tense) of a sentence we change the form of the verb.

Examples Josie **wears** sunscreen. (present tense)

Josie **wore** sunscreen. (past tense)

Josie **will wear** sunscreen. (future tense)

When we write **information reports** we write in the **present tense** and when we write the **pros** and **cons** of a **discussion** we write them in the **present tense** too.

1. These sentences are all written in different tenses. **Name** the tenses.
   - a Yuki swims every day wearing sunscreen. ______________ tense
   - b This summer will be very hot. ______________ tense
   - c The sun burned the tips of my cat's ears. ______________ tense
   - d "Slip, Slap, Slop" is a good skin safety motto. ______________ tense

2. These sentences are all written in the present tense. **Rewrite** them in the **past** tense by changing their verbs.
   - a Maria always wears a T-shirt over her swimmers in the pool.

   ____

   ____

   - b We pitch a tent for shade when we go on a picnic.

   ____

   ____

   - c The day is hot and bright so we wear hats and sunscreen.

   ____

   ____

Punctuation—Possessive apostrophe revision

Can you **help** the artist put his apostrophes in the right place?

a the bees hive

b the yachts sails

c the birds nests

Fun with words

1 Can you **match** these sounds to the summer things that make them?

a dry beach sand		thunder
b high surf		squeak
c waves		suck
d wet beach sand		splash

2 I **rhyme** with ***sister*** and ***mister*** and I am a sign of bad sunburn.
I am a ___ ___ ___ ___ ___ ___ ___.

3 It is a hot, sticky day. Mr Tubb is hot and sticky too. Can you **unscramble** the hot, sticky words for the air around him and the hot, sticky word that describes how his skin feels?

HUDIM ________________ air

GGYUM ________________ air

YEAMST ________________ air

MMCLAY ________________ skin

4 To protect yourself from sunburn at the beach you will find all these useful. **What** are they? You can guess from the rhyming clues.

a I'm a happy rainbow **fella**: U ___ ___ ___ ___ LL ___
b In a tube I have **been**: S ___ ___ ___ ___ ___ ___ ___ N
c I'm a bowler and a beret and a fez but I'm not a **bat**: ___ ___ ___
d T-shirts do not **believe** in me: LONG SL ___ ___ ___ E

Your turn to write

Tip for top writers

When writing pros and cons for a discussion:

- **write** them in order of importance;
- **write** in single sentences;
- **try** to have an equal number of points for both sides;
- **try** to answer the points on one side with points on the other.

1 **Choose** one of these topics for discussion and **write** three points **for** it and three points **against** it.

- Every child should walk to school.
- All boys should play football.
- Everyone should learn to ride a bicycle.
- Students should not watch television during the week.
- Winter school holidays should be longer and summer holidays shorter.

Pros

1. ______________________________

2. ______________________________

3. ______________________________

Cons

1. ______________________________

2. ______________________________

3. ______________________________

2 Now **write** a **conclusion** to your discussion after deciding which points make the strongest case, the pros or the cons.

____

Chapter 9 Writing a procedural recount

A **procedural recount** tells how a procedure (an activity or a process) was carried out in the sequence (order) that it was carried out.

STRUCTURE

LANGUAGE

How we watched roots grow

Introduction (idea and plan)

Mrs Russo told us how plants grow from seeds. Trung wished he could see how their roots grow under the ground so Mrs Russo said we could do an experiment to see them growing. She said we could make a plant viewer.

Procedure steps in sequence

Step 1: the container

She cut the top off a big plastic milk bottle. Then she cut one side off the box-shaped bit at an angle so that part of the bottom got cut off too. This left three sides on a small base.

Time words make sequence clear

Step 2: the clear side

Michael found a clear plastic cooking oil bottle. Susie cut a rectangular piece out of it to use as a clear side for our plant viewer. Then she held the clear piece against the milk-bottle box so Mrs Russo could stick it on with green workman's sticky tape.

Shape adjective

Now our viewer had a see-through side. We filled it up with earth and Renee made it damp with a water sprayer. Then Trung and Lal planted four bean seeds in the earth close to the clear side of the viewer.

Because roots grow in darkness Mrs Russo found some black paper and we cut out a rectangle to hang down in front of the clear side like a curtain. She sticky-taped it across the top so it wouldn't fall off. We put an elastic band around the viewer and the curtain to make sure all light was kept out. Then we put the plant viewer in the cupboard for a week.

Comparison to make use clear

Step 5: put on window sill and water

A week later the bean seeds had sprouted tiny leaves. Because leaves need sunlight to grow green we put the viewer on the window sill. After that we watered the plants every morning with the sprayer.

Factual adjectives

Every second afternoon we lifted the black paper curtain. Through the clear side we could see the bean roots. They were growing straight down the clear side of the viewer as fast as the leaves and the stem grew upwards. The roots were long and thin and white.

Facts only: no imagination

Conclusion

Trung was very proud of what we had done. He gave a talk about our experiment to our school assembly.

What did you read?

1 **Circle** the correct answer. The main task of this text is to recount:

a roots b plants c an experiment about seeing roots grow

2 **Circle** the correct answer. Trung:

a told us how plants grow from seeds
b wished he could see plant roots growing
c said the class could carry out an experiment

3 **Circle two** correct answers. The plant viewing box was made of a:

a plastic milk bottle
b clear plastic soft drink bottle
c clear plastic cooking oil bottle

4 **Why** did the plant viewer have one clear side?

____

5 **Complete** this sentence.

Mrs Russo used the green sticky tape to attach the ______________ to the viewer and to stick the ______________ to the top edge of the viewing side.

6 **Circle two** correct answers. When the experiment was finished, Trung discovered:

a roots grow straight down
b bean roots are green
c bean roots are thin
d roots grow more slowly than leaves and stems

How is it written?

1 **Circle** the correct answer. The subject, an experiment to see plant roots grow, first appears in **paragraph 1/paragraph 2**.

2 The author uses many time words and phrases to show the order in which things were done. **Write** down two time words you find in paragraph 6.

a ______________ b ______________

3 **Circle** the correct answer. This procedural recount contains:

a facts and opinions b facts only c instructions only

4 **Circle** the correct answer. This procedural recount tells how the class made a plant viewer:

a slowly b quickly c in the order they made it

5 **Circle** the correct answer. Which occurs in both the first and the last paragraphs to complete the recount?

a Mrs Russo b the experiment c the idea of seeing how roots grow

Spelling and meaning

experiment	**through**	**straight**	**tape**
view	**cupboard**	**upwards**	**taped**
piece	**leaves**	**plastic**	**tapped**

When a words ends with **~e** then the vowel that comes before it is usually **long** (e.g. t**a**pe). We call this **bossy e** because it tells other vowels what to do. If there is no **bossy e** at the end, then the last vowel is usually **short** (e.g. t**a**p).

1 **Name** the object in each picture and write SHORT or LONG underneath to describe the vowel sound.

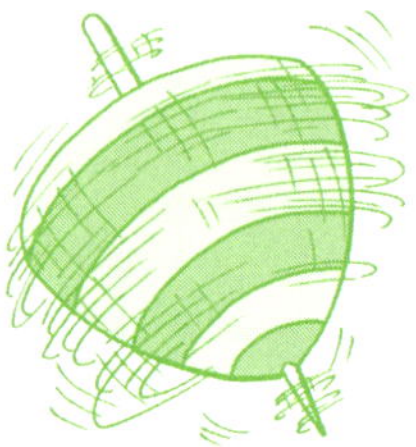

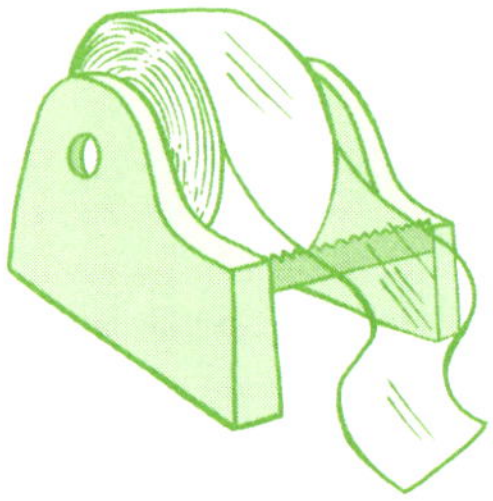

a R____________ b T____________ c M____________ d STICKY T____________

____________ ____________ ____________ ____________

2 When we add ***~ed*** to a **short** vowelled verb we **double** the last consonant (e.g. tap → ta**pp**ed). **Add *~ed*** to each of the following.

a rap ____________ b drip ____________

c map ____________ d sip ____________

3 The word ***cupboard*** contains a silent ***p***. We don't pronounce it. **Underline** the silent letter in each of these words.

a knife b numb c pneumonia d receipt

Some letters occur in groups (e.g. the letters ***ie*** when they make the sound **ee**). Always remember:

I* comes before *E (e.g. believe, piece) **except after *C*** (e.g. receive).

4 **Insert *ie*** correctly **four** times and ***ei*** correctly **once** in the following:

a He sighed with REL ___ ___ F.

b Kelly is Mr Ando's N ___ ___ CE.

c May I have a P ___ ___ CE of that cake?

d This is my REC ___ ___ PT for that book.

e The city was under S ___ ___ GE by its enemies.

5 **Write** a word from the word box to explain these pictures.

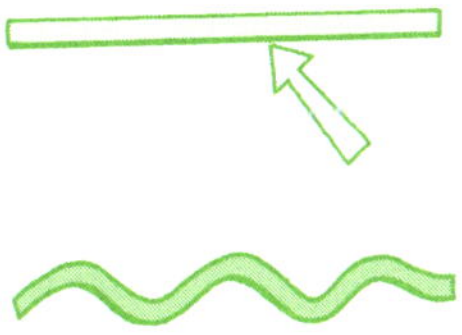

a ________________ b ________________ c ________________ d ________________

Grammar

Adverbs of time (time words) are very important when you are writing a procedural recount. They help the reader understand exactly when things were done.

Example The salt dissolved and disappeared ***after*** I poured water on it.

1 These are common adverbs of time. **Insert** them correctly in the following sentences.

then	when	after	finally	early	before

a ______________ you plant a tree you must dig a hole.

b ______________ the sun sets the sky turns red and gold.

c He planted, watered and fertilised his cornfield and ____________ in summer he harvested it.

d The scientist conducted an experiment, ____________ he wrote a report on it.

e If you look to the west ____________ in the morning you will see the moon setting.

f ____________ the storm the ground was littered with hailstones.

2 **Underline** all the **adverbs of time** you find in these sentences.

a Peter held the jar while Lote filled it with water.
b During the experiment to grow crystals we had to handle the chemicals carefully.
c After we learned about old-fashioned clocks we built a sundial in the playground.
d Please water the seedlings now, before it gets too hot.
e Tonight it will be possible to see a full moon.

3 Look at these two pictures. **Write** a sentence starting with the adverb ***after*** to explain what is happening in them.

Punctuation—Revision

1 **Insert** all missing apostrophes in these contractions.

- **a** Im going, youre going, hes going. In fact, were all going to the Science Expo in the city.
- **b** Wheres the sticky tape to bind up this parcel?
- **c** Theyve all gone to the aquarium to study fish.
- **d** It isnt true that it can rain cats and dogs.
- **e** Weve been collecting money to buy seeds for a class garden.

2 **Insert** all the missing **capital letters**.

- **a** new zealand and norway are both famous for their fiords and glaciers.
- **b** the kalahari, sahara, gobi and atacama are all barren deserts.
- **c** the russian yuri gagarin, in his spacecraft vostok I, was the first man in space.
- **d** astronomers can tell us all about planets like mars, jupiter and saturn.
- **e** the pacific ocean has a powerful influence on the weather of australia.

Fun with words

1 Scientists do lots of experiments to find out how and why things work. The people below are all scientists. Can you **complete** their names?

a G __ __ LOGIST	I study rocks
b M __ __ __ __ LURGIST	I study metals
c CH __ __ IST	I study chemicals
d ENT __ M __ L __ GIST	I study insects
e B __ TANIST	I study plants

2 We are also scientists. Can you **match** us to our field of study?

a astronomer		the oceans and their currents
b marine biologist		volcanos
c oceanographer		the creatures of the sea
d climatologist		the moon and the stars
e vulcanologist		the weather patterns of the world

The clear side of the plant viewer in the text at the beginning of this chapter was described as ***see-through***. It could also have been called a ***transparent*** side.
The prefix ***trans~*** means **through** or **across**. This side could be seen through.

3 Do you **know** these ***trans~*** words?

a TRANSP __ R __ __ T (e.g. window glass)
b TRANS __ C __ __ NIC (e.g. across the Pacific Ocean)
c TRANSM __ T (e.g. to send a radio or television signal)
d TRANSN __ T __ __ N __ L (e.g. a company with branches in many countries)

4 Can you **complete** this scientific explanation?

When light shines through a raindrop or a diamond it creates a rainbow coloured light. Raindrops and diamonds are TR __ __ __ LUCENT. They let light shine through them and break it up into its colours.

5 These are the colours of a rainbow. Can you unscramble them?

a DER: ____________

b GEROAN: ____________

c LLOWYE: ____________

d NEEGR: ____________

e LUEB:

f DIGOIN: IN________O

g TELIOV: V________T

JOKE

Q. What two things can you never eat for breakfast?
A. Lunch and dinner.

Your turn to write

Tip for top writers

When writing a procedural recount:

1 **Stick** to the facts.
2 **Connect** the facts with time words.
3 **Put** the facts in order.
4 **Link** your last paragraph to your first.

1 Professor Schmidt is conducting an experiment. Can you **complete** his explanation of what his experiment proves?

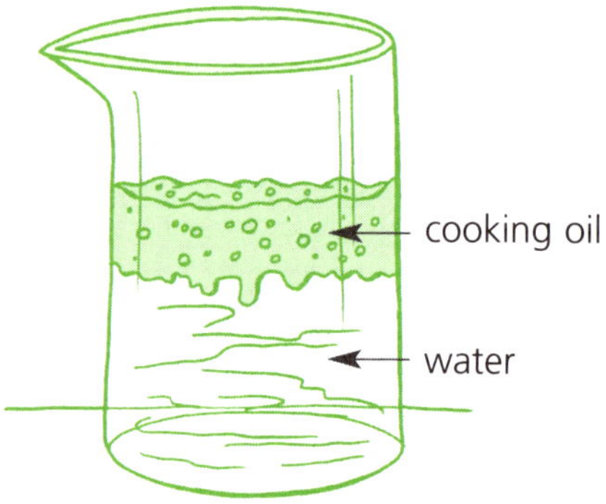

I, Professor Hans Schmidt, have demonstrated that ______________ weighs less than ______________ because, even though I poured it into the glass ______________, it is now floating on top of the water.

2 **Think** about everything Professor Schmidt did to conduct his experiment—the equipment he had to gather, the materials he used, the details of the experiment itself and the order in which he conducted it. Then **write** a procedural recount of his experiment on the following scaffold.

Orientation (What did the professor want to find out?) ______________________

____

____

____

Paragraph 1 (Gathering equipment and materials) ______________________

____

____

____

Paragraph 2 (What the professor did first) ______________________

____

____

____

Paragraph 3 (What he did next) ______________________

____

____

____

Conclusion (What the experiment proved) ______________________

____

____

____

Answers on pages 77–78

Chapter 10 Writing a response to a picture

When we write a **response** to a picture we **explain** what we see and what we **think** and **feel** about what we see.

STRUCTURE

LANGUAGE

Introduction

This photo was taken in Sideshow Alley at a country show. It is a picture of one of the rides. We can see two boys driving a car on the end of one of the arms of a machine.

Body of response

The arms of the machine are raised. The middle bit must be an engine that makes the arms go round and round. It is covered with flashing lights and looks exciting.

Details and response

The ticket office is advertising a special deal of four dollars a ride or four rides for ten dollars. If you pay ten dollars you can ride on the Cup and Saucer, this car ride, the Big Bubble and the motorbikes. The boys probably wouldn't want to ride in a cup and saucer so I think they only paid for one ride.

Details and response

The little cars have headlights like great big eyes and the ticket office is painted with happy pictures. Even though this is not a colour photo I can imagine all the little cars painted in bright colours. All the coloured lights would be flashing red and green and yellow. I am sure there is loud happy music playing as the cars go round. No wonder the boy on the left is smiling.

Details and response

The boy on the right is looking back over his shoulder. Perhaps he is looking at his parents watching him drive. He has the steering wheel so I think he feels very proud of himself.

Conclusion a personal decision

I would really like to go to a show like this one day.

Clear, short sentences

Fact

Opinion

Fact

Opinion

Comparison to make picture clear

Direction to help reader

Writer's own opinion

What did you read?

1 **Circle** the correct answer. Sideshow Alley is:
a a movie theatre
b a street of rides and games at a show
c another name for a country show

2 How much did each boy pay for his one ride? ____________________

3 **Name** two other rides the boys could have chosen.
a ____________________ b ____________________

4 The writer thinks one boy is feeling very proud.
a Do you **agree**? __________
b Can you **explain** why he might feel proud? ____________________

____

5 **Circle** all the correct answers. Looking at this picture makes the writer:
a use imagination
b feel sad
c feel happy
d want to go to a show

How is it written?

1 **Circle** the correct answer.
The first paragraph tells us what is happening in the picture and where it is happening.
True/False

2 **Complete** this sentence.
This response includes both F ___ ___ TS and OP ___ N ___ ONS.

3 **Read** paragraph 2 carefully and then **circle** the correct answer. The opinion sentence in this paragraph is:
a the first sentence
b the second sentence
c the third sentence

4 Directions help the reader see which part of the picture you are describing. **Write** one direction you find in the text.

____

5 **Insert** these verbs in the following sentences to complete the sentence correctly.

thinks	imagines	describes

The writer ____________________ what he sees. He puts himself in the place of the boys in the picture and ____________________ what they must be feeling. He uses his senses to tell us what he ____________________ the colours and the sounds of a show might be.

Spelling and meaning

background	whether	electricity	machine
foreground	weather	power	booth
alley	different	centre	ticket

When learning the words in the word box don't be put off by their size. **Break** them into **smaller words** (e.g. back-ground) or into **syllables** (e.g. el-ec-tric-it-y). Remember every big word is only a group of smaller words or syllables.

1 **Complete** these sentences with a word from the word box.

a The truck is in the ____________________ of the picture.
b The car is in the ____________________ of the picture.

2 **Insert** a word from the word box in these sentences.

a John couldn't decide ______________ to go to the show or the beach.
b If the ______________ is fine the show will be a success.
c Fuad strolled down the narrow winding ______________.
d Lightning is natural ______________ in the air.
e Your prize is ______________ from mine. Mine's a medal but yours is a star.

3 **Which word** from the word box would describe the position of all the arrowed items in these pictures?

____

4 ***Fore*** means **in front**. Can you **complete** these ***fore*** words?

a FORE ___ ___ ___ ___ (part of your face)

b FORE ___ ___ ___ (wrist to elbow)

c ___ ___ FORE (opposite of *after*)

d FORE ___ ___ ___ ___ ___ ___ (lower front of picture)

e FORE ___ ___ ___ (man in charge of a work team)

5 **Circle** the correct answer.

Power and *electricity* can mean the **same** thing. They are **synonyms/antonyms**.

Grammar

Plural subjects (more than one) are always followed by the **plural form of the verb**. **Single subjects** are followed by the **singular form of the verb**.

Examples The crane (singular) is lifting (singular) that car.

The cranes (plural) are lifting (plural) the car.

1 **Circle** the correct answer in these sentences.

a Chloe and Yusuf **is/are** going to the show.

b Little children **is/are** enjoying the cup and saucer ride.

c My dad **is/are** playing Throw the Ring Over Your Prize.

d All the boys **is/are** driving dodgem cars.

When we use a **group noun** to name **one** gathering of people, animals or things, we usually use the **singular form of the verb**. This is because a group noun names **one** group.

Examples The audience (group noun) was (singular verb) silent during the concert.

The fleet (group noun) is sailing (singular verb) south.

2 **Circle** the correct answer in these sentences.

a A crowd of spectators **was/were** watching the Grand Parade.

b A pair of pigeons **is/are** asleep in the rafters.

c A herd of cattle **is/are** to be exhibited in the main arena.

d A clutch of chickens **is/are** on display in the poultry shed.

3 **Read** these sentences carefully and then **circle** the correct answers.

a Claudia and Aldo **is/are** playing a piano duet.

b That swarm of bees **is/are** nesting in the roof of the ticket booth.

c Mrs Leonello **make/makes** delicious fairy floss.

d A team of horses **is/are** pulling a wagon of hay.

e Twelve boys **is/are** lined up to buy dodgem car rides.

Punctuation—Revision

Insert all the missing punctuation. (Think about capital letters, commas and full stops.)

one of the great shows of the world is the calgary stampede in canada. it is an exhibition of cattle horses and horse-riding skills. every year people come from as far afield as argentina australia new zealand the united states and even mongolia to compete in the calgary stampede. they pit their skills against each other in competitions like rounding up roping cattle and riding bulls. in addition to the cattle and horse events there are all the usual show activities including displays of local produce exhibitions of local craftwork and all the games and rides of sideshow alley

Fun with words

1. Shows usually include a display of produce—grains, fruit and vegetables grown locally. **Sort** these produce items into the right barrows.

wheat	bananas	potatoes	barley	grapes	strawberries	carrots	millet
pineapples	rye	pumpkin	squash	lettuce	cabbage	rice	lemons
beans	mangoes	corn	pears				

2. These are all berries. Use the clues beside them to **name** them.

a B ___ ___ ___ ___ BERRY (I rhyme with ***tack***.)
b B ___ ___ ___ BERRY (I am the colour of very cold hands.)
c S ___ ___ ___ ___ BERRY (I am what's left after wheat is harvested.)
d R ___ ___ ___ BERRY (It's not polite to blow me.)
e B ___ ___ ___ ___ ___ BERRY (I sound like boys 'n girls.)

3 Country shows also feature judging of farm animals. Can you **unscramble** these animals listed for judging?

a SPIG ______________ b PEESH ______________ c TTCAEL ______________

d TOAGS ______________ e CHKNSIEC ______________ f SHSOER ______________

4 I'm a new animal at country shows. My homeland is South America. I am an A ___ P___CA.

5 To **complete** the show title that everyone wants to win you must throw the balls into the clown's mouth and choose which lanes you want them to land in. **Choose** the correct lanes by **letter** and you will be able to complete the title.

GRAND C ___ ___ ___ ___ ___ ___ N

6 You will find us at a show. **What** are we?

a A vertical turning wheel of chairs: I am a F ___ R ___ ___ S WH ___ ___ L.
b A sticky pink fluffy sweet: I am F ___ ___ ___ Y F ___ ___ SS.
c Little cars that bump into each other: We are D ___ ___ G ___ M C ___ ___ S.
d Displays of fruit, grain and vegetables: We are PR ___ D ___ ___ E.

Your turn to write

Tip for top writers

When writing a response to a picture:

- **Write** the place (and the time, if you can).
- **Write** what is happening (facts).
- **Write** what you think (opinion).
- **Write** any conclusion (wish, decision) you reach.

1. Look closely at this picture.
   a. Make a **list** of **facts** (what you see in the picture).

   b. Make a **list** of your **thoughts** about the picture (e.g. Would you like to be there? Are the people happy?).

   c. **Write** a **where/when** introduction to your response.

   d. **Write** a conclusion to your response, saying whether you would or would not like to do what the people in your picture are doing. Explain why you think that.

2. Using all your answers to question 1, **write** a **response** to your picture on your own paper. Remember to file it carefully in your folder.

Answers on pages 78–79

Chapter 11 Writing for school research projects

When we write a **biography** we are recounting the **life** and **achievements** of someone. A **time line** records the same information in a **visual** way.

The biography

Shirley Smith (Mum Shirl)

Shirley Smith was an Aborigine of the Wiradjuri people of New South Wales, Australia. She was born in Cowra in 1924 and lived there till her family moved to Sydney when she was a young woman.

In the late 1930s she began to visit people in gaol because she knew they were lonely and had no one to talk to. She kept visiting them when they came home from gaol and helped them find work and places to live. She became known as Mum Shirl by all the people she helped.

At the same time Mum Shirl began to take into her own home children who were unhappy or homeless or whose parents were sick. Over her lifetime she was mother to over sixty children.

Because she saw the need for better services she was one of the people who set up the Aboriginal Medical and Legal Services in 1971 and 1972. Her work for other people was tireless.

In 1985 Mum Shirl was awarded an Order of Australia in recognition of her lifetime's work on behalf of people in need. When she died in 1998 thousands of people from all walks of life felt they had lost a friend. They felt they had been privileged to know a truly good person.

The time line

Life of Mum Shirl

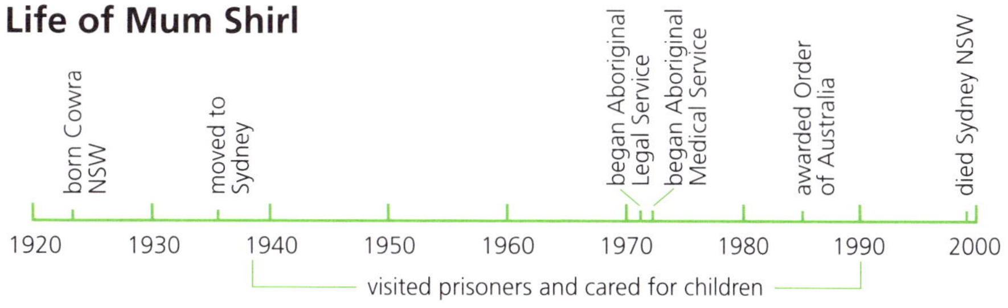

Biography or time line? What are the differences?

1 **Complete** this sentence.
A biography is written in S ___ NT ___ ___ CES and a time line is written in short PHR ___ SES.

2 **Circle all** the correct answers. In a biography key points are:

- a dates of birth and death
- b colour of shoes
- c places of birth and death
- d dates of important events in life
- e family and friends
- f favourite song
- g opinions of others
- h personality

3 **Circle** the correct answer.
Both biography and time line are arranged in chronological order (order of events). **True/False**

4 **Circle** the correct answer.
The time line and the biography **do/do not** contain exactly the same information.

5 Which writing allows you to say what other people think about your person, the biography or the time line? ______________________

6 Sometimes it is not possible to find out exactly when something happened in your person's life. In this case would you write a biography or a time line? ________________

7 If you were writing about an inventor who invented something new every single year, would it be more sensible to write a biography or a time line? ____________________

8 **Complete** the following sentences.

a A ________________ allows us to see the span of someone's life at a glance.

b A ________________ lets us find out what someone did during his or her life and why and how they did so.

Your turn to write

Tip for top writers

When you write a biography:

- **Use** your own words (do **not** copy straight from a book or the Internet).
- **Include** important dates and places.
- **Write** events in the order they occurred in your person's life.
- **Explain** why your person is important.

1 **Write** a short biography of someone in your family, starting with their birth and ending with who they are and what they are doing now.

Date and place of birth ______________________________

____

Main events in life ______________________________

____

____

____

____

____

____

How you feel about this person ______________________________

____

____

2 **Complete** a time line of your own life starting with your birth.
Use the time line below and mark on it the dates that are special in your life.
Then write above those dates what happened then to make them special.
Each space represents one year. The first will be the year you were born (and wasn't that a great year!).

Answers on pages 79

Answers

Chapter 1 Pages 2–7

What did you read?

1 False
2 b
3 c
4 a
5 d
6 The end of a glacier is tall and flat-faced like a wall. It is all blue-green ice.
7 The brown streaks are made by the earth the glacier travelled through.

How is it written?

1 yesterday, today, tomorrow
2 crossed, drove, stopped, looked, stayed, bought
3 black and white pictures
4 They are green-brown/They are vicious/ They rip up soft parts of cars/They let down tyres

Spelling and meaning

1 a bought
b peek
c diary
d tyres
e peak
f dairy

2 a N
b N
c N
d Y

3 ER: herd, fern; IR: whirl, bird; UR: fur, furl; EAR: heard, pearl

4 a pearl
b heard
c furl

Grammar

1 a Glaciers **are** rivers of ice.
b Harry **climbed** the glacier wall.
c A glacier climber **carries** rope, spikes and a small hammer.

2 a The waters of mountain lakes are very cold.
b Snowboarding and skiing are popular sports in the Alps.
c Mountain air is very thin.

3 a Glaciers carry stones in their ice but rivers carry silt in their waters.
b Glaciers begin in alpine lakes but rivers begin in mountain rains.
c Thin ice looks white but thick ice looks blue or green.

Punctuation

Some mountains are famous for their snow, mountains like **E**verest in **N**epal, **F**uji in **J**apan, the **M**atterhorn in **A**ustria and **T**ongariro in **N**ew **Z**ealand. **O**ther mountains like **M**t **S**t **H**elen in the **U**nited **S**tates, **V**esuvius in **I**taly, **P**inatubo in the **P**hilippines and **G**unung **A**gung in **I**ndonesia are volcanic and famous for boiling lava and explosions.

Fun with words

1 mild, cool, chilly, cold, icy

2 a cool
b icy
c cold

3 a glacier
b lake
c billabong
d tide

4 a skis

b sled
c toboggan
d chair lift

5 mountain goat

Your turn to write

1 1. wake
2. wash
3. dress
4. eat
5. clean teeth

2 1. Dog chased my cat
2. Cat raced up tree
3. Cat wouldn't come down
4. I climbed tree
5. Cat climbed higher
6. I climbed higher
7. Both too frightened to climb down

Chapter 2 Pages 8–15

What did you read?

1 False
2 The 19th Battalion of Chocolate Wheatens
3 The Wheatens and the Tim Tams
4 defeats
5 c
6 a
7 b

How is it written?

1 a
2 sequence
3 headquarters, regiment, battalion, division
4 a, c
5 a

Spelling and meaning

1 a bis/cuit
b i/cing
c fal/ter
d dec/lar/a/tion
e de/ci/sive
f use/less

2 a armour, biscuit, capital
b dangerous, defeat, division
c 1. biscuit 2. bow 3. gun 4. shield
d siege, sign, single
e decisive, declaration, falter, useless, weapon

3 a capital, capital
b headquarters
c weapon
d falter

4 a humour
b clamour
c vigour

Grammar

1 a abstract
b group
c group
d group, abstract, group

2 a mob
b pack
c fleet
d school
e congregation

3 a generosity
b leadership
c mercy
d courtesy

Punctuation

a Is India north or south of the Equator**?**
b Good heavens**!** That pink pig is flying**!**
c Chile's flag is sky blue with a big yellow sun in the middle**.**
d What is the national language of Brazil**?**

Fun with words

1 a pride
b clutch
c congregation
d swarm
e pack
f team

3 a admiral, captain, seaman
b principal, deputy, teacher, student
c prime minister, minister, member of Parliament

Chapter 3 Pages 16–21

What did you read?

1 a
2 In the packet of grass seeds there must also have been weed seeds.
3 The cat ate him because he was too fat to run away.
4 in Ryde
5 a
6 apple cider
7 c
8 She was so thin she slipped down her straw into the lemonade.
9 birds

How is it written?

1 person
2 a, b
3 Ryde, died, inside

Spelling and meaning

1 a flea
b flue
c flaw
2 sneak, spy, tattle, rob
3 a creep
b rob
c sneak
d watch
4 a ferment
b either
c pain
d wren
e beard
5 a wrench
b wring
c wrong
d write
e wriggle
6 a white
b dry
c cloudy
d going
e full

Grammar

1 a tall, thin, red, baggy
b skinny, bandy, round, little, round, black
2 a lonely, jolly
b selfish, happy
c thoughtful, kind
3 a visible, invisible, naked
b ripe, unripe
c venomous, harmless

Punctuation

1 isn't, don't
2 haven't, She's

Fun with words

1 a tickles
b funny
c head
d spinning
2 a gyring, gimbling
b wabe
c brillig
d slithy
5 a clown
b magician
c ventriloquist

Your turn to write

1 ramble
2 a Who went for a ride on a tiger
b Who sported an awful black shiner
c Who only ate water with bran

Chapter 4 Pages 22–27

What did you read?

1 action
2 a nectar and pollen collecting

b making honey

3 False

4 She is too big.

5 Nurses

6 b

7 what it eats

How is it written?

1 hives are not dome-shaped/queen lives in bottom storey/queen cannot enter other floors/queen is bigger than other bees

2 nectar/pollen/drone/sacs/nurse/queen

3 a, c

4 shape, colour, size, number

Spelling and meaning

1 a collect
  b pollen
  c communicate
  d entrance
  e dome

2 a horses
  b fish
  c pigs
  d cows
  e geese
  f koalas

3 a creatures
  b storeys
  c burrows
  d hives
  e hatcheries
  f hutches

4 a source of underground water
  b male pig
  c female horse
  d town leader
  e passenger boat
  f tiny invisible creature with wings

Grammar

1 a build
  b hibernate
  c are
  d is
  e watch

2 a were sunning
  b is resting
  c were hunting
  d was cruising

3 b hibernate
  c defend

Punctuation

a Ants stand guard, hunt, trap, build, climb and migrate.

b Pandas are only known for sleeping, eating and sleeping again.

c Dolphins are famed for diving, leaping out of the water, barrelling and somersaulting.

Fun with words

1 a nestling
  b calf
  c cub
  d fingerling
  e calf
  f cygnet

2 owl, possum, racoon, bat, jaguar, fox, mouse

3 a eyrie
  b warren
  c mound
  d lair

Chapter 5 Pages 28–33

What did you read?

1 c

2 a

3 a dust
  b cobwebs

4 It smelt like sunshine and grease and wood shavings all mixed together.

5 wait

6 His grandfather didn't like him standing around doing nothing.

How is it written?

1 b
2 b, c
3 c
4 a, c
5 adjectives

Spelling and meaning

1 a straight
  b weight
  c label
  d idle
  e sneeze
2 grease
3 a wait
  b peal
  c reeds
  d reel
  e pail
  f real
  g peel
4 a crooked
  b cry
  c busy
  d demolish
  e open

Grammar

1 a complex
  b compound
  c compound
  d complex
2 a (Unless there is a breeze) the paint won't dry.
  b (While we were in the old shed) we saw a redback spider.
  c (Even though there were cobwebs in the attic) we were not frightened.
3 a Unless it is raining I will go to the bakery.
  b Although it is so old, the school still has not fallen down.
  c When you are here we will paint the fence.

Punctuation

1 a "Does dust make you sneeze?" Ibrahim asked Paul.
  b "Hand me some more nails," the carpenter told his apprentice.
2 a "Help!" he shouted. "The wind is lifting the roof off!"
  b "I know you like the beach," said Melissa, "but I prefer the mountains."

Fun with words

1 a bottles
  b comics
  c lamps
  d tools
2 a lighthouse
  b igloo
  c mosque
  d observatory
3 a hammer
  b saw
  c screwdriver
  d spanner
  e chisel
5 a plum
  b bob → plumb bob

Chapter 6 Pages 34–39

What did you read?

1 Year Four
2 a bright colours
  b loud music
3 a laziness/bad attitudes
  b swearing
4 False
5 d

How is it written?

1 I believe
2 b

3 b
4 Cartoons are violent/Bugs Bunny and Road Runner show an average of 55 violent acts per hour.
5 Dr Patricia Edgar/The International Coalition against Violence
6 a, c, e

Spelling and meaning

1 a break into a conversation
 b between countries
 c between states
 d point where two roads meet
 e come between two quarrelling people
 f get in the way of someone and their work
2 a telescope
 b television
 c telegraph pole
3 a community
 b influence
 c negative
 d extremely
 e international

Grammar

1 a early
 b eagerly
 c usually, very
 d cheaply
 e positively
2 a today (when)
 b usually (when)
 c there (where)
 d internationally (where)
 e negatively (how)

Punctuation

[I firmly believe that if you have a pet you should look after it as if it is a member of your family. After all, it lives in the same house as you and shares every part of your life, probably even more closely than your friends do.
[So what does looking after your pet like family mean? First, it means your pet is fed daily. It means it is fed what is right for its breed, not just scraps from the kitchen. It means you make sure it has plenty of clean fresh water to drink every day.
[Like us, pets feel the heat and the cold. In winter you must make sure it has a warm dry shelter out of the wind and rain and in summer you must see that it has lots of cool shade to protect it from the heat.
[If it is sick you take it to the vet and if it is miserable you play with it and reassure it that it is your friend. We owe our pets the same loyal friendship they give us.

Fun with words

1 a story in cartoon format
 b serious, acted story about people and events
 c program discussing real events and issues
 d how to improve your life, house, garden, holidays
 e program designed to make you laugh
 f competition with competitors and prizes
2 1. village, 2. town, 3. city, 4. metropolis
3 a rather
 b very
 c extremely
4 a mixed adults
 b an ambassador
 c your football team
 d a judge
 e a minister called Smith

Chapter 7

Pages 40–45

What did you read?

1 b
2 a
3 c
4 a It clogs the breath.
 b It stings the eyes.
5 It damages its parts.

6 The topsoil, which is the good growing soil, has been blown away.

How is it written?

1 True
2 A dust storm is a moving wall of dust.
3 Red dust has been blown onto New Zealand's snow.
4 largest, smallest
5 problem

Spelling and meaning

1 a travelling
b moving
c proving
d labelling
e deciding
2 a a long time without rain
b make
c occasionally
d without covering
3 a invisible
b inaudible
c intangible
4 a inaudible
b invisible
c intangible
5 a draw
b drawer
c bear
d bare

Grammar

1 a absolutely
b less
c very
2 a wildly
b tomorrow
c very

Punctuation

1 a farmer's
b plant's
c India's and Australia's
d meteorologist's
2 a birds'
b horses'
c Farmers'

Fun with words

1 a arid
b barren
c dusty
d thirsty
2 dry, dusty, cracked, hot, burning, bare, arid, empty, dead, thirsty, wilted, bony, dying, hungry, withered, dry
3 a camel
b oasis
c date
4 a hurricane
b cyclone
c tornado
d gale
e typhoon
f thunderstorm

Chapter 8

Pages 46–51

What did you read?

1 c
2 cancer
3 a
4 The UV rays of the sun burn the skin until it turns red and blisters.
5 a silly point because it distracts the audience from important arguments
6 b
7 all the time we are outside

How is it written?

1 strongest
2 for, against
3 strongest to weakest
4 a
5 can

Spelling and meaning

1 a sunscreen, discussion, cancer, continually, colouring, protect, protection, conclusion
  b cancer
2 a soft
  b soft
  c hard
  d soft
  e soft
  f hard
3 a likely
  b protect
  c continually
  d wear
  e cancer
4 a discussion
  b argument
  c protection

Grammar

1 a present
  b future
  c past
  d present
2 a Maria always **wore** a T-shirt over her swimmers in the pool.
  b We **pitched** a tent for shade when we **went** on a picnic.
  c The day **was** hot and bright so we **wore** hats and sunscreen.

Punctuation

a bees'
b yachts'
c birds'

Fun with words

1 a squeak
  b thunder
  c splash
  d suck
2 blister
3 **Air:** humid, muggy, steamy; **Skin:** clammy
4 a umbrella
  b sunscreen
  c hat
  d sleeve

Chapter 9 Pages 52–59

What did you read?

1 c
2 b
3 a, c
4 To allow the students to see what is inside.
5 Mrs Russo used the green sticky tape to attach the **clear side** to the viewer and to stick the **curtain** to the top edge of the viewing side.
6 a, c

How is it written?

1 paragraph 1
2 A week later/After that/every morning
3 b
4 c
5 b

Spelling and meaning

1 a rope (long)
  b top (short)
  c mop (short)
  d tape (long)
2 a rapped
  b dripped
  c mapped
  d sipped
3 a **k**nife
  b num**b**
  c **p**neumonia
  d recei**p**t
4 a relief
  b niece
  c piece
  d receipt
  e siege
5 a upwards

b straight
c through
d piece

Grammar

1 a Before
b When
c finally (*or* then)
d then
e early
f After

2 a while
b During
c After
d now, before
e Tonight

3 After he read about the moon in a book the boy went outside and looked at the moon through a telescope.

Punctuation

1 a I**'**m, you**'**re, he**'**s, we**'**re
b Where**'**s
c They**'**ve
d isn**'**t
e We**'**ve

2 a **N**ew **Z**ealand and **N**orway are both famous for their fiords and glaciers.
b **T**he **K**alahari, **S**ahara, **G**obi and **A**tacama are all barren deserts.
c **T**he **R**ussian **Y**uri **G**agarin, in his spacecraft **V**ostok I, was the first man in space.
d **A**stronomers can tell us about planets like **M**ars, **J**upiter and **S**aturn.
e **T**he **P**acific **O**cean has a powerful influence on the weather of **A**ustralia.

Fun with words

1 a geologist
b metallurgist
c chemist
d entomologist
e botanist

2 a the moon and the stars
b the creatures of the sea
c the oceans and their currents
d the weather patterns of the world
e volcanoes

3 a transparent
b transoceanic
c transmit
d transnational

4 translucent

5 a red
b orange
c yellow
d green
e blue
f indigo
g violet

Your turn to write

1 I, Professor Hans Schmidt, have demonstrated that **oil** weighs less than **water** because, even though I poured it into the glass **first**, it is now floating on top of the water.

Chapter 10

Pages 60–66

What did you read?

1 b
2 four dollars
3 Cup and Saucer/motorbikes/the Big Bubble
4 a Yes
b Because he is the driver of the car.
5 a, c, d

How is it written?

1 True
2 facts, opinions
3 b
4 on the right
5 The writer **describes** what he sees. He puts himself in the place of the boys in the picture and **imagines** what they must be feeling. He uses his senses to tell us what he **thinks** the colours and the sounds of a show might be.

Spelling and meaning

1 a background
  b foreground
2 a whether
  b weather
  c alley
  d electricity
  e different
3 centre
4 a forehead
  b forearm
  c before
  d foreground
  e foreman
5 synonyms

Grammar

1 a are
  b are
  c is
  d are
2 a was
  b is
  c is
  d is
3 a are
  b is
  c makes
  d is
  e are

Punctuation

One of the great shows of the world is the **C**algary **S**tampede in **C**anada**.** **I**t is an exhibition of cattle**,** horses and horse-riding skills. **E**very year people come from as far afield as **A**rgentina**,** **A**ustralia, **N**ew **Z**ealand, the **U**nited **S**tates and even **M**ongolia to compete in the **C**algary **S**tampede. **T**hey pit their skills against each other in competitions like rounding up, roping cattle and riding bulls. **I**n addition to the cattle and horse events there are all the usual show activities**,** including displays of local produce**,** exhibitions of local craftwork and all the games and rides of **S**ideshow **A**lley.

Fun with words

1 **Fruit:** bananas, grapes, strawberries, pineapples, lemons, mangoes, pears; **Grain:** wheat, barley, millet, rye, rice, corn; **Vegetables:** potatoes, carrots, pumpkin, squash, lettuce, cabbage, beans
2 a blackberry
  b blueberry
  c strawberry
  d raspberry
  e boysenberry
3 a pigs
  b sheep
  c cattle
  d goats
  e chickens
  f horses
4 alpaca
5 Grand Champion
6 a ferris wheel
  b fairy floss
  c dodgem cars
  d produce

Chapter 11 Pages 67–69

Biography or time line? What are the differences?

1 sentences, phrases
2 a, c, d, e, g, h
3 True
4 do not
5 the biography
6 a biography
7 It would be sensible to write a biography because a time line would be too crowded. You would not mention every invention.
8 a time line
  b biography

Notes